NO PLACE LIKE HOME

NO PLACE LIKE HOME
INTERIORS BY MADELINE STUART

[signature]
5 Oct 2019

PHOTOGRAPHY BY TREVOR TONDRO
FOREWORD BY MAYER RUS

Rizzoli
NEW YORK

New York Paris London Milan

To my parents, who set me on my course.
To Steve, who encouraged me along the way.
And to the clients who gave me the chance.

CONTENTS

FOREWORD

I've been badgering Madeline Stuart to do a book for years. But every time the subject arose, my dear friend would always trot out the same argument. "Henri Samuel doesn't have a monograph," she'd say, referring to the late, legendary French decorator. "Who am I to do a book?" This was invariably followed by a screed against upstart designers who have the chutzpah to publish self-congratulatory panegyrics with nothing but a few apartments and a pop-up shop under their belts.

Happily, in 2018, a definitive monograph on Samuel finally hit the bookshelves, and either by design or happenstance, Madeline decided that the time had come to do a book of her own. It was worth the wait. Presented here, for the delectation of true aficionados of design, are eight of Madeline's most toothsome projects, each a master class in the fundamentals of scale, proportion, color, texture, craftsmanship, composition, and form. The mix is a testament not merely to her virtuosity as a decorator but also to her dexterity in conjuring eminently compelling interpretations of styles ranging from Spanish Colonial and Streamline Moderne to Arts and Crafts and Mountain Modern.

Long before the terms *authentic* and *immersive* became hackneyed marketing cant, Madeline's interiors were precisely that. They proclaimed their authenticity sotto voce, in their materials and construction methods, in their fastidious marriage of vintage and contemporary furnishings, and in the connoisseurship and imagination that brought them to life. As for being immersive, Madeline would be the first to condemn—publicly, if necessary—any interior that fails to meet that standard.

Which brings us to the subject of her extraordinary candor. Madeline is a Savonarola of style, a latter-day prophet, a magnificent messianic figure, inveighing against the hypocrisies of our time (to borrow a phrase from Paddy Chayefsky). In the decorator demimonde of air kisses and other artificial niceties, Madeline calls it like she sees it, ever steadfast in her belief that style untethered to substance is meaningless.

Given the current state of the design world, where pop stars are held up as tastemakers and Pinterest scavengers masquerade as professional decorators, Madeline's insistence on the old-school virtues of design artistry and craft is all the more refreshing. And although she has proven herself more than adept at pressing her case through writing and rhetoric—as this volume amply demonstrates—it is ultimately her work that speaks most eloquently about the power and magic of great design. Welcome to Madeline's world of wonder.

—*Mayer Rus*
Los Angeles, California

INTRODUCTION

In order for me to tell you something about myself, I need to tell you about my parents, who are ultimately the shapers of my vision and the molders of my persona.

My mother was the style maker. A designer of note in her own right, she taught me about fashion and taste, which she displayed effortlessly in the way she dressed, in the way she decorated our house, and in the way she entertained. She believed in timelessness above all else and had a way of combining clothing and jewelry, art and furniture, modern elements and antiques—all with an understated flair. I can't say for certain if I inherited her instincts or if I absorbed them by osmosis, but to this day she has a profound influence on the way I see, interpret, and experience beauty.

My father was the teacher. He was maniacal in his efforts, and some of my earliest memories are of Sunday afternoons when he taught my brother and me the distinctions between Bach and Beethoven, the meaning and wordplay of a Shakespeare couplet, or the subtle elegance of Gershwin melodies and Miles Davis riffs. Our bedtime stories were lessons in history; I'm unclear as to why, but the story of Sir Walter Raleigh and the Spanish Armada was a particular favorite for him. My father loved novels and nonfiction, science and chess, music and film, art and theater. (The first movie I ever saw was Laurence Olivier's version of Shakespeare's *Henry V.* I was six.) My father was insanely passionate about what was to be revered—and what should be dismissed—in a way that did not permit discourse or disagreement. (I'm afraid I'm a bit too much like him when it comes to issuing decrees as to what's good and what's simply dreadful.)

The house I grew up in established my penchant for interiors that feel authentic and appear somewhat undecorated. My childhood home was Spanish Revival in style, built in the 1930s. It had elaborately patterned wood floors, frescoes on the ceiling, a seventeenth-century Italian fireplace, and a swirling stair railing of wrought iron. There was a pair of exceptionally beautiful two-story stained-glass windows in the foyer, and the living room featured a large bay window with a grid of leaded and colored panes of handmade glass. (We lived in fear of our father's wrath should an errant ball do irreparable damage.) My mother was an instinctive mixologist, combining English and French antiques with contemporary art, comfortable sofas, and modern lamps. The decor was warm, inviting, and classic, but not specific to any time or place. The living

room was used for living, the dining room for dining. There was no designated "family room," the all-too-common catchphrase for a space adjacent to the kitchen where an enormous TV screen holds center stage. We played in our rooms or went outside. No toys were permitted downstairs—Draconian conditions by today's standards.

I didn't have much say when it came to my room. My mother was the decider, and one day I came home to find the walls covered in a white Brunschwig & Fils wallpaper scattered with small red and pink flowers—I never cared for it. My antique four-poster bed was festooned with a canopy of dotted Swiss—a fabric not much in vogue these days—and there was a vintage wicker desk and a Victorian-era wicker rocking chair, both painted white. In the original red-and-black tile bathroom she hung framed pages from Ludwig Bemelmans's marvelous *Madeline* books, including the one that read "To the tiger in the zoo / Madeline just said, 'Pooh-pooh.'" My sentiments, exactly.

Over time I put my teenage stamp on the room, replacing the desk with an architect's drafting table, taping posters over the wallpaper, and installing a supermarket shopping cart filled with my record collection. I surely thought my alternative use for that purloined wagon was truly inventive—and no doubt my mother was horrified. I would love to say my design career started when I decorated my childhood bedroom, but that's definitely not the case.

The most direct route from one point to another is normally described as a straight line—that's not my story. Mine was a circuitous path, with many detours. It took years of flailing about—trying on different professions as though they were shoes—before I discovered my true calling. How I envied those who knew right from the start who they were destined to be.

There was time spent running a business (into the ground, by the way) selling rare and collectible records. I sold test pressings and bootleg recordings by Bowie, the Stones, and Dylan to obsessive collectors in the United States, Japan, and Europe, and I sent a copy of The Beatles' *Yesterday and Today* "butcher" cover to some guy in Sweden. I loved the music but resented the fact that I worked alone in an office over Walter Keller's golf shop on Westwood Boulevard.

After that there was a stint in the food industry (prepackaged pâté anyone?) and an attempt to snag a job in the promotions department at Columbia Records (it seems I didn't score high enough on the typing test). I thought about going back to school to become a psychologist (a degree that would serve me well in my current profession), and at one point I even considered going to work at the Los Angeles Zoo. (Did you know you need to pass a civil service exam for those positions?) Newly married and intent on finding my way, I recognized I couldn't make a living as an artist, but felt certain that whatever I did would have to engage and explore my creative instincts.

As it so happened, a childhood friend was the one who finally set me on the right road. Someone she knew—a young screenwriter—had landed himself a terrific apartment, but he was at a complete loss as to how to furnish the place. I recall that he had a futon on the floor, a pitiful orange lamp, and a Barcalounger (do they still make such things?) in the empty living room. I had less than zero experience and nothing to offer other than my mother's resale certificate and a sense of what would be appropriate, comfortable, and affordably stylish.

I outfitted his pad with an upholstered bed, some great-looking lamps, and the modernist's answer to a recliner, the iconic Eames lounge chair and ottoman. I was immensely proud of my first effort, the client was satisfied, and he was quick to recommend me to his friends. In biblical fashion, that job begat the next, which begat the next, and so on.

Before I knew it I had a thriving business catering to the young and restless Hollywood crowd. Up-and-coming producers, agents on the rise, and junior studio executives populated my client roster. My career as an interior designer was thus created. At times I regret not having apprenticed with an established firm, and I'm a bit chagrined that I plunged headfirst into this field without the benefit of a design mentor. I learned the hard way—the trial-by-fire method. My knowledge was acquired through doing, along with lessons learned as a result of minor (and occasionally major) mishaps. It's not a route I would recommend to anyone.

From the beginning I was a fervent reader of shelter magazines—I still mourn the demise of *House & Garden*—and I obsessively collect books on architecture, design, and the decorative arts. Although the Internet is certainly a valuable resource, most of my inspiration and ideas still come from my library. And of course from the movies.

I grew up in an industry town, and as a showbiz kid, Hollywood's output was a part of my life. Most Saturday nights were spent watching old movies on television or in the home-screening rooms of family friends. I was infatuated with classic films from the 1930s and '40s, and surely my affinity for the interiors of that period were forged by the countless movies I saw starring

Fred Astaire, Cary Grant, Bette Davis, Claudette Colbert, and William Powell. (If you've never seen the screwball comedy *My Man Godfrey*, I highly recommend it—not only for the costumes and performances but also for the sheer fabulousness of the sets.)

For those who aren't aware of my own film history, I have a brief—but critically important—screen appearance in *Willy Wonka & the Chocolate Factory*, a film my father directed. The original book by Roald Dahl was one of my favorites, and I begged my father to make it into a movie. In addition to my fifty-dollar finder's fee, I was rewarded with a single line of dialogue in the classroom scene. (I say, "About a hundred.") Tragically my film career was short-lived—I have no other credits to my name. But the experience of spending months on the *Wonka* set at Bavaria Studios was absolutely magical. Every time a client walks into their house for the great unveiling, their look of joy and amazement reminds me of that moment in the movie when Wonka opens the door and the lucky winners get their first glimpse of the chocolate factory.

For all the study, experience, and exposure, I must admit that my real education has come from working with—and for—my clients. The best ones encourage and support my creativity. They provide me with the opportunity to express new ideas and grant me permission to

My brother, Peter (dressed for his gig as a stand-in for Mike Teavee), and me on the set during the filming of *Willy Wonka & the Chocolate Factory*.

explore myriad solutions. I've learned to consider opposing notions graciously and am now capable of allowing my initial design concept to go in a completely different direction. I'm eternally grateful to the clients who collaborate with me to find the most beautiful outcomes. Truth be told, even the difficult clients—the combative sort challenge me to discover something I might not have otherwise seen.

Although my interiors have appeared in numerous magazines, I was initially resistant to memorializing them in a book. For years I maintained that celebrating a designer's oeuvre should be reserved for those who had racked up a body of work after decades of dedication to the craft. Well, those criteria now apply to me. "The time has come," the Walrus said . . .

For this book, my first, I have selected eight residences, each one representing a specific aesthetic. In nearly every instance, the design directive was dictated by the architecture as well as the site. All of the projects I've included are ones in which I worked closely with the clients. In each case, these are people who live in and love their homes—these interiors are not set designs created for the camera, and there are no velvet ropes barring entry. And although the eight projects are distinctly different, I like to think that aspects of each link them together, even if I can't say for certain exactly what those elements are.

After numerous clients and countless projects, I've learned to trust my instincts. I'm now confident I have a style that's uniquely my own. I'm neither a traditionalist nor a modernist. I've come to respect and embrace design from virtually all periods (although, truth be told, I'm not a big fan of the Memphis mash-up look) and delight in being able to cull and place objects from disparate regions and eras, just as my mother had done in my childhood home. I love working with tile installers and textile artists, upholsterers and cabinetmakers. Every facet of the work I do is akin to reinventing the wheel, each time out. But that's what makes it interesting—never doing the same thing twice, never allowing the look of my last project to dictate the ideas for the next. My love of design, art, and architecture is what guides and sustains me. Perhaps it's precisely because I took a meandering path that I now fully appreciate the opportunity I have to see and create beauty in the world.

When the filming of *Willy Wonka* wrapped, my father gave me a locket with the following inscription: "We are the music makers. We are the dreamers of dreams."

The line wasn't in the book—it was written by the poet Arthur O'Shaughnessy—and it was my father's idea to include it in the film. Wonka may utter the words, but it's my father's directive—and his artistic credo—that I try to put into practice every day.

BY THE SEA

Virtually the only thing worth keeping was the Moorish-inspired arch on the front facade. This striking architectural detail was original to the house, built in 1922 by an early land baron in the California beach town of La Jolla.

Much had been altered during the intervening years. Native son and longtime owner, actor Cliff Robertson, installed a hodgepodge of cheap Mexican tiles and made numerous architectural blunders, yet the house was considered a historic property. That designation meant that, although renovation was possible and additions to the footprint would be allowed, the front facade had to remain exactly as it appeared in a vintage photograph—the only source material that showed the building in its original state.

Thus that distinctive Moorish arch informed, influenced, and dictated almost every decision I made regarding the architectural design and decoration of the house.

Hispano-Moresque architecture is not uncommon in Southern California, and its signature flourishes are evident on buildings throughout the United States. Prominent Florida architects Addison Mizner and Maurice Fatio were early enthusiasts, and exceptional examples are on the East Coast and, somewhat surprisingly, in the Midwest.

The style's emblematic attributes emerged during the seven-hundred-year period when Spain was dominated by North African Berbers, who brought with them such Islamic-based design elements as elaborate tiles and plasterwork, intricate geometric decorative motifs, and ornately carved wooden doors. Married with traditional Spanish architecture, the union produced exceptional buildings and details that celebrate both cultures.

It just so happened that I'd visited Morocco a few weeks prior to starting this project, and I'd become obsessed with everything Moroccan—architecture, embroidery, tile work, textiles, food! Less than a year later I made the pilgrimage to Spain to visit the Alhambra in Granada—a holy site for Hispano-Moresque acolytes. I also traveled to Ronda and Seville, wandering awestruck through gardens and buildings that reflect a strong Moorish influence. I'd acquired the educational equivalent of a starter kit, and I couldn't wait to incorporate what I'd seen and learned into the design of this house.

The client's directive was simple: This was a beach house, after all, and it needed to feel like one. Nothing too dressy, nothing too formal. Architectural aspirations notwithstanding, the place had to welcome friends and family who would travel here for fun and sun.

Our goal was to create a house that embraced the elemental qualities of the Hispano-Moresque style without resorting to ironic decorative gestures. The place needed to look as

OPPOSITE: A detail of the exceptionally intricate inlay on an eighteenth-century Spanish table in the living room. FOLLOWING SPREAD: The front facade of the house had to remain due to its historic status. Although restored, it looks as it did when the house was built in 1922. The tiles we found for the fountain date to the sixteenth century, and the stone basin in the center is from the nineteenth century. Brian Tichenor of Tichenor & Thorp Architects designed the landscape.

though it belonged to an earlier time but with a modern sensibility. It should be playful but calm; incorporate color but remain somewhat neutral; and, above all, feel accessible but unconventional.

As always, I started by compiling a dossier of inspirational imagery. My office library is a nerd's answer to Pinterest, and my staff and I pored over scores of books that focus on all aspects of Spanish and Moorish architecture and Islamic decorative arts. I'd taken umpteen photographs while on my various trips, and we organized them by topic: ceilings, tile patterns, window grilles, clavos-studded doors, and so on. We accumulated hundreds of images, and we used them the way you'd incorporate words while learning a new language—they became flash cards that represented the vocabulary for the house.

We began with the bathrooms: thirteen in all. We determined that the cabinetry and light fixtures would be unique to each and that most would feature fabulous patterns of classic *zellij* tiles, which are still made in Morocco. (The Islamic-based geometric patterns of *zellij* tiles integrate thousands of different shapes and motifs, creating seemingly endless varieties.) The bathrooms feature different colored tiles—navy and white, black and white, turquoise and white. Elaborate yet surprisingly simple, these rooms were exceptionally fun to create.

Designing the ceilings in the house presented more of a challenge. Some are all plaster with run-in-place moldings—a detail that's sadly becoming increasingly rare. (In fact very few new houses incorporate true plaster, and to see it being applied is a thrill, if you like that sort of thing.) The two largest spaces—family room and living room—have intricate ceilings fabricated entirely of wood. The most difficult ceiling to construct, however, was the one we designed for the homeowner's office—it combines plaster with a complicated pattern of interlacing wood beams.

To balance the elaborate ceilings, we created interior doors and cabinetry with extravagant patterns that integrated custom moldings and carved detailing. The door hardware was inspired by 1920s Spanish Revival knobs and levers that we found at a source for vintage hardware in Los Angeles. We tweaked the design of the originals and had our versions cast in bronze. Every cabinet pull was carefully considered, and what we couldn't find we designed and had custom made.

We discovered a fabulous antique fireplace mantel for the living room and commissioned a talented stonemason to make the one in the owner's study. Other fire surrounds in the house were fashioned out of plaster, which is appropriate for a home of this type and period. Humble in terms of material yet highly decorative, a plaster mantel can feel understated yet elegant, the equivalent of a perfect piece of jewelry.

OPPOSITE: The entry foyer embraces a mix of cultures, countries, and architectural influences. Ancient Roman artifacts and an Arts and Crafts–period Japanese bronze vessel rest on the nineteenth-century Italian marble console. The ceiling is hand-formed plaster, and the terra-cotta floor tiles were custom made. The iron mirror is by French designer Raymond Subes, and the alabaster chandelier is from France; both date to the 1930s. The chair is nineteenth-century Spanish and is upholstered in a gauffraged velvet by Venice-based textile artist Sabina Fay Braxton.
FOLLOWING SPREAD: A vintage iron-and-glass lantern is the centerpiece of a ceiling crafted from butternut wood. The works of art are by Frederick Hammersley (over the fireplace) and Richard Diebenkorn, and the Italian mantel dates to the nineteenth century.

ABOVE: A dramatic black-and-cream Spanish Prado carpet was one of the first pieces purchased for the house; its graphic quality provides a punch to the otherwise muted color scheme.
OPPOSITE: I love quirky lamps, and the copper-and-tole confection on the demilune table is a perfect example. The mirror is nineteenth-century Italian and features a faux tortoiseshell frame.

This project was a perfect opportunity to pursue my passion for finding antique and vintage lighting. I located fixtures all over the country from sources both grand and not-so-grand. I turned up the perfect pair of sconces for one of the bathrooms in a junky antiques shop—they would require nickel plating and rewiring, but their funky condition didn't deter me from imagining them in their much-improved incarnation. I found the living room's spectacular iron-and-glass lantern at auction. In New York, I came across a set of four vintage carved-alabaster sconces for the master suite and paired them with an elaborately carved-alabaster pendant that crowns the bedroom. (I didn't have to travel far to find that piece—it was waiting to be discovered at a dealer's shop just up the street from my office.) We ultimately hunted down and installed more than two hundred distinctive light fixtures for this house.

The intention was to convey a light and beachy feel, so I selected a palette of varying shades of taupe, beige, flax, sand, and wheat. I also incorporated a range of whites, offset by blues that range from sea glass and turquoise to teal and navy blue. Soft black (I refer to it as John Singer Sargent black) is perfect for the study. A hit of terra-cotta brightens up the family room. But other than these, I kept the hues restrained so as not to distract from or compete with the intensity of the ever-changing colors of the ocean. In order to prevent an overwhelming blandness, I used textiles and carpets that balance smooth textures with rough, as exemplified in the coarsely woven grass matting in the gallery or the handwoven patterns of the drapery panels in the family and living rooms. I selected and designed rugs to carry the textural weight of the rooms, so color wouldn't have to do the heavy lifting.

This house was many years in the making, and over the course of the project I sought out furniture that was authentically Spanish in origin. A few Italian antiques are scattered throughout, but the majority of the eighteenth- and nineteenth-century pieces come from Spain. Even the Cuenca tiles surrounding the fountain in the center of the front garden are Spanish, created more than four hundred years ago. And although it's not imperative that a French house contain French furniture or an English house feature English furniture, it was satisfying to place so many Spanish pieces in these rooms. Their presence provides an element of authenticity that resonates with the prevailing architectural style, and their patina radiates a warmth and beauty only acquired over time.

At one point during construction, the original Moorish arch and the flanking walls were the only part of the house left standing—a few strategically placed boards held them up like the facade of a Hollywood film set. (You walked through the front door and nothing was on the other side except the view.) In remodeling and reimagining this house we sought to respect the vision of the 1922 structure as well as its historical antecedents. I wanted this place to feel old and new at the same time, without resorting to design trends or bowing to contemporary tastes. So much of what's built today feels temporary—how grateful I am to have a client whose mission was to create a home not only for family and friends but also for generations to come.

I placed a collection of 1930s copper and bronze vessels on a nineteenth-century Italian sideboard.

OPPOSITE: Bianco Nuvolato marble lines the wall of the powder room adjacent to the office. The marble sink is vintage, and the mirror is eighteenth-century Flemish. FOLLOWING SPREAD: The ebonized Berber chairs, two of my first purchases for the house, pair beautifully with a stunning nineteenth-century Oushak carpet. The abstract painting above the custom stone mantel is by Lee Mullican, and the ceramic plate is by Pablo Picasso. PAGE 32: The client had a cache of old-growth walnut that was used to make the cabinetry we designed for the office. PAGE 33: Gutsy and decidedly masculine, the French desk from the 1960s is made of stitched leather with an iron base.

PRECEDING SPREAD: The loggia's dining and seating areas—as well as the Pacific Ocean—beckon beyond the forty-foot-long gallery hall. The stone consoles are eighteenth-century Italian, and the works of art are by Andy Warhol. RIGHT: The Richard Misrach photograph of waves was an obvious choice for this seaside house. The walnut-and-iron dining table was custom designed as were the chairs, which have a matte-gesso finish. The plaster ceiling with an elaborate geometric pattern was handmade and installed piece by piece.

ABOVE AND OPPOSITE: The family room's plaster fireplace features a vintage Gladding McBean glazed terra-cotta tile inserted above a mosaic of *zellij* tile. The urns at the end of the gallery hall are eighteenth-century Spanish. FOLLOWING SPREAD: We designed an elaborate wood ceiling in the Hispano-Moresque style for the family room. The trestle table is eighteenth-century Spanish, and the iron lamps are also Spanish, from the 1930s.

PAGE 42: The design of the family room ceiling is based on classic Islamic geometric motifs, a hallmark of Hispano-Moresque architecture. PAGE 43: A collection of vintage Mexican copper vessels is arrayed on the eighteenth-century Spanish table in the family room. OPPOSITE: Classic Drucker bistro chairs provide a jolt of color in a kitchen that features walls of *zellij* tiles in an icy blue-white hue.

ABOVE: When I found this mother-of-pearl tile, I knew I wanted to use it floor to ceiling—it makes a stunning backdrop for a custom marble sink stand with vintage nickel legs and the vintage shell sconces. OPPOSITE: In another bathroom, the sink cabinet is Syrian dating to the early nineteenth century, and the Arabesque sconces are from the 1920s.

ABOVE AND OPPOSITE: It's a challenge to find eccentric and unique antique lighting; these remarkable iron fixtures are the spoils of a victorious search. We had 1920s tiles—from the Grueby Faience Company—set into the plaster risers of the staircase.

A remarkable example of Anglo-Indian artistry, this nineteenth-century four-poster bed is made from solid rosewood. The mirror is from the 1960s and was created by Mexican architect and designer Arturo Pani, and the bedside tables are nineteenth-century Italian.

OPPOSITE: A pair of custom chairs covered in a hand-woven fabric of angora wool provides a quiet moment in the master bedroom sitting area. The side tables are Italian circa 1880, and the shell sconces and chandelier are vintage alabaster. ABOVE: A chest of ebony, mother-of-pearl, and tortoiseshell is Spanish Colonial in style, but is from Mexico and dates to the nineteenth century.

ABOVE: The design of the master bathroom's marble floors was inspired by a pattern I'd seen in Morocco.
OPPOSITE: The antique marble tub is positioned to take optimum advantage of the glorious view. The silver-plated sconces and nickel-plated ceiling fixtures are from the 1930s.

OPPOSITE: I found a gorgeous Moroccan rug, but it was much too big; so I had it cut in half in order to make it work in two guest bedrooms. The elaborately carved wood bed was actually a pair of twins that we had cojoined to make it a king size. ABOVE: A Portuguese-style ebonized bed is the star of this guest room. The view through the French doors is of the front garden with the ocean in the distance. Custom embroidery on the curtains and Roman shades creates a different look in each room, in spite of the same carpet underfoot.

We designed each one of the thirteen bathrooms to be unique. Patterns and colors vary, but many of them are unified by the use of traditional Moroccan *zellij* tile.

The Pacific Ocean may beckon just beyond the lawn, but for many the pool is the preferred spot for a swim. Sitting atop the stucco walls is a collection of vintage glazed urns from the 1920s and '30s, whose colors are echoed in the custom tiles of the pool's interior.

MOUNTAINS MAJESTY

I was warned at the outset that this was possibly the ugliest house in Jackson, Wyoming. Nonetheless, it was situated in the best location in town: high on a ridge overlooking the Snake River with views of the Teton Range stretching from north to south. Not a single obstacle blocked the purple mountain majesties.

As bad as the exterior was, the interiors were even worse. The house was designed in the 1970s, and the concept of perpendicular walls was clearly anathema to the architect. Whether it was personal taste or the era's vogue for angles and asymmetry, the anxiety-inducing rooms felt pinched and compromised. (Never mind that it's extremely difficult to furnish a space shaped like a tortilla chip.)

When my co-conspirator and collaborator, the brilliantly talented David Lake of San Antonio-based Lake|Flato Architects, first saw the property, he lobbied for demolition. But my client had other ideas. Thus began a twelve-year odyssey of intermittent construction, with breaks for planning, permitting, drawing, and designing—all timed so the family could hold their traditional gathering every year between the twentieth of December and the second of January.

The initial directive was to bring order to the madness of the architecture. To start, we undertook a preliminary round of painting, tiling, carpentry, and furnishing, finishing in time for the family's first Christmas get-together at the house.

There's no arguing that one of the most common sights in Jackson is the log cabin on steroids. Houses of twenty thousand square feet are standard issue, and most are furnished in a manner that suggests a lack of imagination. From the start we set out in a different direction, one that didn't conform to the conventional wisdom for Jackson Hole interiors. No plaid. No red. No antler chandeliers. No furniture made from logs or wagon wheels. We wanted to explore juxtapositions of modernity and warmth, refinement and comfort, a simple palette while eschewing beige. And with all due respect to the master interpreter of Western Style, we were determined to avoid the well-worn Ralph Lauren–inspired fantasies.

A vintage decorative object of repoussé copper hangs in the family room's inglenook.

In an effort to create a uniquely personal style for this house, we decided to include vintage pieces that conferred a note of modernity to the interiors. We relied on exceptional works by midcentury masters. The entry is anchored by a Paul McCobb bench covered in sheepskin, and a pair of T. H. Robsjohn-Gibbings wood-frame armchairs completes the seating arrangement in the living room. We surrounded a table of striped wood by Milo Baughman in the library with eccentric Don Shoemaker chairs that feature slung leather seats. Hans Wegner designed the chairs in the breakfast area. In the bedroom sitting area, a fabulous table made of slate, metal, concrete, and iron by Dutch furniture artisan Paul Kingma rests between his-and-her chaises longues.

These were conscious choices, but it was absolute serendipity that led me to a showstopper: a Philip and Kelvin LaVerne table, which I knew instantly was meant for this house. Covered with an abstract representation of a forest, the patinated bronze coffee table became the focal point of the living room's fireplace inglenook.

Initially, paint made the biggest difference. When full-on remodeling is not an option, a gallon of paint and a brush can have a profound impact. In this house, color authority Donald Kaufman's palette quieted the angles and calmed the spirit of the interiors with shades that respect the natural environment. I incorporated sage greens for doors and baseboards, muted khakis in the hallways, and a subtle ochre for the walls of a bedroom. Common beadboard wainscoting installed over the drywall provided texture and depth in many rooms. Cheap and cheerful, this classic paneling was an easy fix for a lifeless space.

We specified squares of dark brown cork flooring throughout the lower level. Durable, sustainable, and super chic, cork is warm and sound absorbent and works virtually anywhere. (Richard Neutra and Rudolph Schindler were both early champions of the material and used it everywhere—even in bathrooms.)

Removing and replacing the house's 1980s-era cabinet hardware also made a profound difference. Often overlooked and ridiculously easy to rectify, outmoded cabinetry can be transformed by the perfect handle the way the perfect pair of shoes can change your life. (Well, that's my theory.)

With bare walls begging for mercy (and not much in the way of a budget for artwork), I headed to one of my favorite resources: the antiques mall. There I discovered midcentury woodblock prints, starving-artist abstracts, and scores of vintage postcards of Jackson Hole.

Moss rock—common in this part of the West—was used for both interior and exterior walls. The light fixture hanging over the entrance is made of slag glass and dates to the 1970s.

RIGHT: A wall of slatted wood conceals the staircase to the loft library. The entry hall's chandelier—a cast-bronze sculpture of a branch that we had wired for electricity—hangs above a shearling-covered bench by Paul McCobb. FOLLOWING SPREAD: Moss rock, a low stained-wood ceiling, and painted-oak walls create a cozy inglenook off the double-height living room. The lounge chairs were custom made for the house and surround a vintage table by Philip and Kelvin LaVerne.

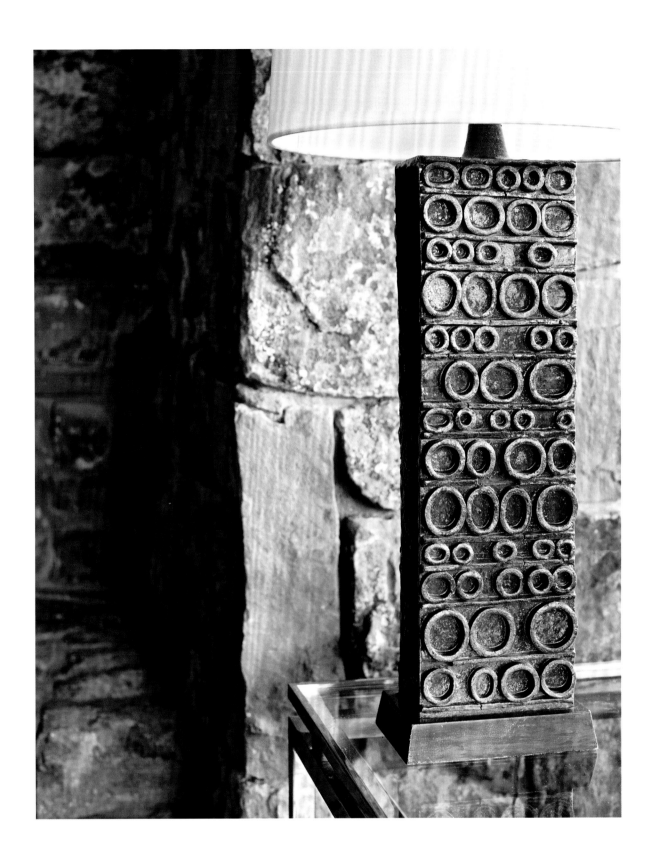

OPPOSITE: The abstract pattern of a forest on top of the LaVerne table made it an obvious choice for a house that looks out over—and is surrounded by—thousands of trees. ABOVE: I love finding unusual things, and this unique lamp incorporates a piece of 1970s art pottery. FOLLOWING SPREAD: The living room is essentially a glass-enclosed tree house that captures exceptional views of the Snake River and the Teton Range in the distance. The chairs in the foreground are vintage T. H. Robsjohn-Gibbings, and the custom area rug is made up of squares of sheared fur.

With their oversaturated colors and charming imagery, these period postcards are winkingly nostalgic. I had them framed in plain dark wood with extra-wide mats—another cheap and cheerful fix—and hung them en masse down hallways and in bathrooms. (I even admit to buying two cornball paint-by-numbers Western scenes that I just couldn't resist.) I discovered a cache of vintage schoolroom maps, which found their way to the bunk room. All these years later, with its bright red metal beds and scattered fluffy lambskin rugs, the space is still a coveted guest room for kids.

Most significantly, we painted the exterior in Benjamin Moore's Texas Leather, a dark muddy green. The previously stark-white structure now virtually disappears into the tree line—when you raft down the Snake River and look up at the house, it is no longer an eyesore on the landscape.

Although we went far afield to find furniture with a modernist sensibility, we respected the spirit of true cowboy culture, incorporating leather, elk skin, fur, hair on hide, sheared lamb, curly lamb, goatskin, and antelope. Just so textiles wouldn't feel left out, we used mohair, wool sateen, boiled wool, coarsely woven silk, and, for good measure, some natural linen.

After the first Christmas, my clients initiated a major round of construction. The focus was primarily on the kitchen and dining area—we eliminated some inexplicably angled walls, squared off rooms, and established a vocabulary of materials that would ultimately tie the entire house together. We installed wide horizontal lap-and-gap paneling of whitewashed oak and Western red cedar. (The contractor balked when I chose to paint over the oak, but I wanted the texture of the boards to telegraph through the paint. The results are subtle but remarkably effective.)

Tackling the remodeling of a house in phases is fairly common—not everyone has the budget or stomach for nonstop construction. Because these clients were determined to spend the holidays in Jackson, we scheduled the work accordingly. A year after the first round, planning was underway for the second assault—the center section of the three-story house would be "surgically" removed and replaced. At one point that winter, you exited a door off the dining room, walked across a plank above a giant chasm, and re-entered through another door that took you to the bedroom wing. Midnight excursions to the kitchen were cold and treacherous.

It's almost inconceivable that someone would design a house with million-dollar views yet position windows so low in the walls that stooping was required to catch sight of the Tetons.

PRECEDING SPREAD: In the kitchen both the walls and the cabinetry are made of the same wood, but milled in a different manner. The cabinets are stained rift oak, while the walls are plain sliced oak that's been painted. Vintage Hans Wegner chairs surround the kitchen breakfast table, and the pottery on the counter is by ceramicist Miri Mara.
OPPOSITE: A Milo Baughman table and quirky chairs with slung leather seats by Don Shoemaker are positioned in the loft library, a secluded reading space above the living room.

ABOVE AND OPPOSITE: Without question, this steel-and-glass extravaganza is one of the most spectacular fixtures I've ever installed. Although we discovered it in San Diego, the chandelier, which weighs nearly three hundred pounds, was made in the 1970s by an artist who was based in Arizona. FOLLOWING SPREAD: A massive room for entertaining, the Party Barn is the latest (and presumably last) addition to the house. An elaborate steel truss is offset by wood-planked ceiling and walls. Along with a pool table, TV seating area, a table for card games, and a full-service bar, the room also offers a glass-roofed deck that provides an unparalleled view up and down the Snake River Valley. PAGE 82: Ceramics are the accessory of choice for the Party Barn. A wall hanging, ceramic rings, and a pair of pierced ceramic lamps are displayed throughout the room. The various tables are cast bronze; one features a top of petrified wood. PAGE 83: The walnut pool table was custom made. The flooring throughout the Party Barn is stained concrete.

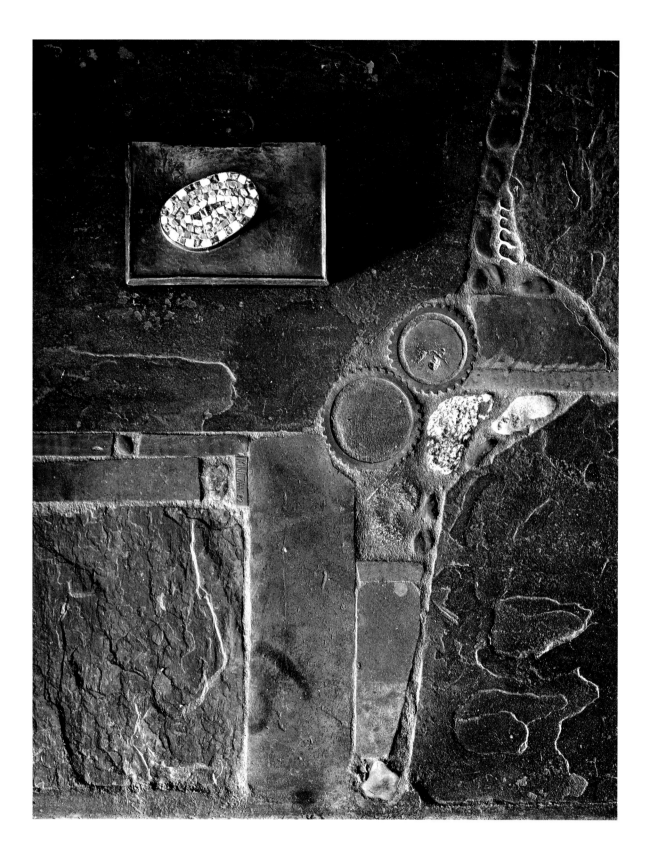

PAGES 84 AND 85: A patinated-bronze panel from the 1970s was created by Philip and Kelvin LaVerne and hangs on the wall in the master bedroom sitting area. The piece holds special meaning for the clients, who are devoted riders. ABOVE: The Dutch furniture artisan Paul Kingma is noted for his brutalist tables, assembled from various materials such as concrete, slate, stone, bits of industrial metal, and pebbles. This piece dates to the 1970s. OPPOSITE: A pair of suede-and-shearling chaises faces the fireplace in the wood-paneled sitting area of the master bedroom. The rug is made from Mongolian lamb, and the curtains are in a handwoven wool by Hiroko Kitada.

But that's indeed what the house's original architect did. David rectified this. He expanded the second-story living room so it cantilevered beyond the existing structure. The result: a modernist tree house, with floor-to-ceiling windows on three sides. The entire Snake River Valley is now in full view, Tetons included. The entry, neither grand nor formal, features stacked moss rock and a wall of horizontal planking that conceals the stairway to a loft library, a secluded nook for reading and musing that we added over the living room. A glassed-in staircase on this side of the house provides access to the revamped lower level where kids can congregate and guests can retreat.

For a time, there was a lull in building, but my clients ultimately recognized that in order to realize the full potential of the house and property they had to embark on a last round of demolition and construction. The scope of this final phase was extraordinarily ambitious and would take more than three years to complete. It involved tearing down the right and left wings of the structure and rebuilding both from the ground up.

The master suite—minimally altered during the first go-round—is now a wood-paneled refuge, with horizontal boards of walnut that we echoed in stone in the bathroom. On this side of the house the redesign included a sitting area and lower office, a wine cellar, and a private porch that provides the perfect perch for eagle watching.

Opposite the master wing is what David terms the Party Barn, a mammoth room for entertaining that serves as a magnet for family and friends. (At the inaugural New Year's Eve party, so many guests were dancing that the area rug buckled in half from all the happy feet.) A screened-in porch for summer dining was added along with a stairwell that offers stunning views. In this two-story space we installed one of our best finds, a one-of-a-kind, artist-made light fixture that dates to the 1970s. More sculpture than chandelier, this ten-foot-high behemoth required special bracing in the ceiling to support its substantial weight. It's one of my favorite fixtures—ever.

Throughout it all, the Christmas tree has gone up and come down, season after season, without fail. This house has been a work in progress for well over a decade. Toddlers are now teenagers; young children are now young adults. My clients didn't want to miss an opportunity to bring everyone together for the holidays, and amazingly enough, they didn't.

PRECEDING SPREAD: With a view that spans the entire Teton Range, the master bedroom is a spare and cozy refuge, situated at the far end of the house. OPPOSITE: Ancient grinding stones were stacked one on top of another to create a table. The art pottery vase was a fortuitous find at an antiques mall in Pasadena. FOLLOWING SPREAD: I designed the stone paneling in the master bathroom to echo the patterning of the wood-planked walls that are a thematic motif throughout the house. Above the stone is a grass-cloth wall covering that creates a virtually seamless transition. The cabinetry is rift oak, the floors are stained concrete, and the ceiling fixture is vintage.

RIGHT: The house lacked an outdoor dining area, so a deck was added during the last round of construction to provide a screened-in room for summer entertaining. A massive board-form concrete fireplace anchors the opposite end of the space. FOLLOWING SPREAD: In what was previously an overgrown and undeveloped area, a steel firepit now draws people to the western edge of the property.

DREAM HOUSE

Walk down almost any street in Los Angeles, and you're sure to find examples of Spanish Revival architecture.

Influenced by the humble white-stucco farmhouses of southern Spain, the style emerged in the early part of the twentieth century as the preeminent building type in Southern California. Such houses tend to be defined by asymmetric facades, arched windows and doorways, interior courtyards, and red-tile roofs. Whether a single-story bungalow or a *casa grande*, the architectural vocabulary of the Spanish Revival style is a fundamental part of the Los Angeles landscape.

But as often happens with architectural archetypes, the specific details that constitute the idealized representation of this form have, over the years, been compromised and misinterpreted. As a result, what tends to be built these days in the so-called Spanish Revival genre is a mishmash of references. Attention is no longer paid to the subtle flourishes prevalent in the 1920s and '30s when the best examples of this style were constructed.

It was imperative to my client that his house—which was to be newly constructed from the ground up—embrace and celebrate the essential characteristics of Spanish Revival architecture. The goal was to create a residence that was so convincingly authentic that few would be able to discern the date of its creation. (Shortly after we finished the project, a gentleman approached me at a party at the house and said he remembered going there as a child.)

My client hired Kevin A. Clark to create his dream house, which is accordingly named El Sueño. Kevin's design incorporates all the hallmarks of the style, with every detail rendered in his singular, hand-drafted architectural drawings. The client insisted on employing the building methods and materials that would have been de rigueur in the 1930s—plaster walls, hand-wrought ironwork, elaborate ceilings, and beams carved with framing chisels, remarkable tools that have been around for centuries but are now rarely used because they're considered to be too dangerous.

With construction underway, my role was to establish an idiom for the interiors that honored and respected the authentic quality of the exterior. I felt it was important to carry the theme throughout the entire residence, manifested in the stone and tile, furniture, rugs and fabrics, and, of course, the lighting. The elements we selected create a harmonious whole that suggests the past but is clearly of the present. Wherever—and whenever—possible, we found antique and vintage pieces that would provide authenticity.

Detail of the fourth-century AD Roman mosaic panel that was incorporated into a custom coffee table for the living room.

Designed by Kevin A. Clark in 2007, the architecture of El Sueño references the classic Spanish Revival residences from the 1920s and '30s that are found throughout Southern California. The house is so convincingly authentic that many who visit are certain it dates to an earlier period.

Our initial task was to design the bathrooms (all eighteen of them!), and we knew that choosing the correct materials would be critical in terms of conveying a 1930s aesthetic. Bathrooms from that period—especially in Los Angeles—are famous for their exuberant use of tile, often in shades of Ming green, shocking pink, or radiant purple, all contrasted with black, a common combination at the time. We located a supplier that made faithful reproductions of tile from that era. For one bathroom, I had them copy a decorative tile from the house I grew up in. (My childhood bathroom, which dated to 1930, was a riot of red and black glossy tile—I am fairly certain that my personality was shaped by that combination.)

For the master bathrooms, we used marble for the wainscot and floors. The approach for these spaces, sophisticated and elegant, seemed more appropriate than using period-inspired tile. His bathroom—a quietly masculine space created from black and gold marble—features commanding vintage sconces from the former Alfred I. du Pont estate in Jacksonville, Florida. Her bathroom is decidedly more feminine, a coral and cool gray confection with an intricate mosaic floor that took nearly a year to make.

One of the unique aspects of El Sueño is the work of decorative artist Jean Horihata. Jean and I have collaborated on numerous projects over the years, but this commission proved to be both a challenge as well as a rare opportunity to showcase her talents on so many aspects of the design. Many rooms in the house display her artistry (the dining room walls, the border in the library, the ceiling of the family room), but the tour de force is the main powder room. It took nearly six months to design this space that was inspired by—and is an homage to—Sir Frederic Leighton's nineteenth-century London house; it took another six months to paint. Leighton's Islamic-tiled hall is festooned with his exceptional collection of sixteenth-century Turkish tiles. We set out to re-create the myriad Iznik designs, rendered entirely in trompe l'oeil. Each faux tile on the walls of the two chambers that make up the powder room was hand-painted then "grouted" to look as if they'd been set in a bed of mortar. Afterward Jean glazed them to approximate the glossy sheen of actual tile. Both magic and talent are required to fool the eye and by my estimation, the result is more amusing than the real thing. (The man who installed the mirror over the sink insisted that he couldn't drill through the tile without using a special bit—despite being told repeatedly that the walls weren't ceramic tile but painted plaster.) Without question, this is my favorite room in a house of many wonderful rooms.

Though not the case on most projects, we started this one with the rugs (in some instances, the cart does come before the horse). A magnificent Persian Bakhtiar from the 1920s determined the palette for the living room (terra-cotta and varying hues of blue), an antique Agra set the tone for the dining room (citrine yellow combined with fuchsia),

The two-story entry is grounded by an elaborate marble floor of our design and crowned by a late seventeenth-century Genovese chandelier. The chest is seventeenth-century Italian, and the contemporary painting is by John Virtue.

ABOVE: A John McLaughlin painting hangs above an eighteenth-century Indo-Portuguese chest on stand. OPPOSITE: A nineteenth-century settee and eighteenth-century Italian chairs provide intimate seating at the far end of the living room. The circa-1920s torchères are the work of noted German metalsmith Oscar Bach. FOLLOWING SPREAD: The living room's mantel is nineteenth-century Italian and was found the same day the contractor was scheduled to install one that was designed and carved for the room—fortunately that mantel was a perfect fit for the loggia fireplace. The mosaic top of the coffee table dates to the fourth century AD, and the gilded chandelier is eighteenth-century Italian.

ABOVE: A striking portrait by one of my favorite painters, the Dutch-French artist Kees van Dongen, is positioned above a nineteenth-century Italian commode in the dining room. OPPOSITE: Carved stone columns frame the view from the hallway into the dining room. The walls were hand-painted in classic Chinoiserie style by decorative artist Jean Horihata. FOLLOWING SPREAD: The Clubhouse was designed to approximate the look of a Prohibition-era speakeasy. The dramatic focal point of the room is the magnificent antique bar that we found in Argentina. French in origin, the bar is from the 1920s and has a marble base, zinc counter, and the original refrigerator doors on the back side. The vintage leather seating is by Frits Henningsen, and the coffee table was designed by Arturo Pani.

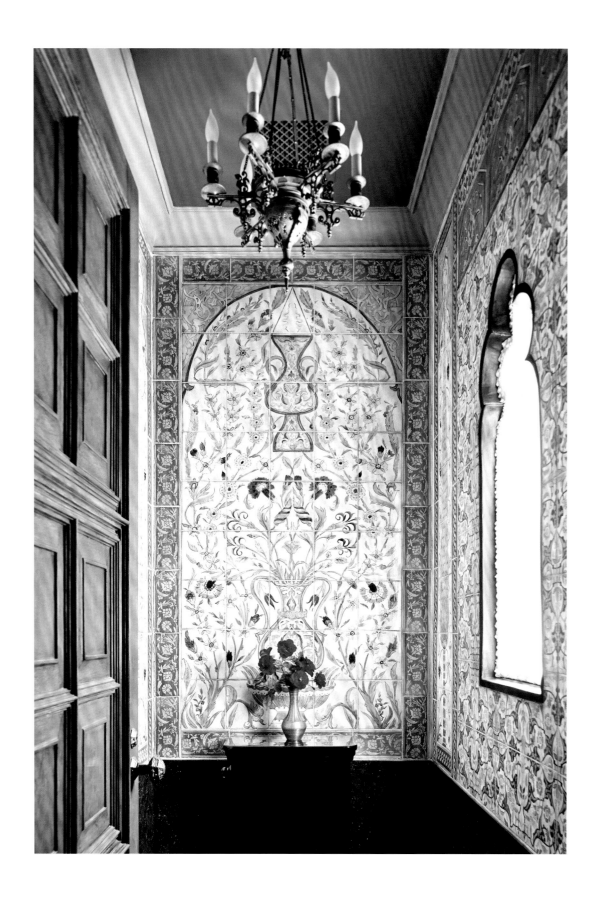

ABOVE AND OPPOSITE: A tour de force of trompe-l'oeil artistry, the powder room was painted to look as though we had installed individual antique Iznik tiles. The walls were then faux-grouted and lacquered to approximate the quality and shine of glazed tiles, some of which are even deliberately "chipped" to look old. It took decorative artist Jean Horihata nearly six months to complete the room.

and a fabulous non-matching pair of Spanish Prado rugs created the backdrop for the master bedroom suite (pinks and greens). We incorporated colors that were saturated but not bright, deep but not muddy. We chose textiles that would hold their own against the architectural weight of the rooms—velvets of cotton, silk, and linen; woven patterns; silk damasks; printed cottons; and Fortuny fabrics. Each room tells a different story through various hues and textiles, yet a continuous thread unites the house.

The first piece of furniture I purchased for this project was for the owner's study: a desk designed by master cabinetmaker Jules Leleu in the 1950s for the director of a French bank. An exceptional example of his later work, it is one of two Leleu treasures in the house—the other is the 1930s coffee table of wood, bronze, and glass in the library. Rather than be bound by a specific period, we incorporated pieces from disparate eras, ancient to (almost) modern. I created a coffee table out of a Roman mosaic mural that dates to the fourth century AD, and the Frits Henningsen chairs in the Clubhouse are from the 1940s. Antiques give the house its soul while pieces from the more recent past provide visual élan.

My obsession with vintage lighting was put to the test on this project—in the end we found, sourced, discovered, and installed nearly four hundred fixtures. Spanish lanterns, ironwork sconces, and alabaster bowls are featured alongside fixtures in gilded tole or intricate bronze. The pair of Italian chandeliers in the dining room was a fabulous find, utterly charming with their gilded wood beads and little nuggets of crystal, and I adore the pair of nineteenth-century German silver fixtures with their original passementerie tassels in the library. But the pièce de résistance, in my mind, is the spectacular three-tiered glass-and-bronze chandelier in the entry. Italian, from the late seventeenth century, it hovers over a floor we designed with rays of Inca Gold, Petit Granite black, and Rosa Verona marble. It's mated with a pair of magnificent crystal-and-bronze Baguès sconces from the 1950s that flank the front door. Though the range of lighting is remarkably varied—and each one is unique—the pieces play well together.

Finding furniture, rugs, lighting, and accessories for a house of this size and scope is unquestionably a challenge, but I'm well suited to the role of hunter-gatherer—I was born to shop, being my mother's daughter after all. It's a victory to locate the perfect piece, uncover a hidden gem, or rout out buried treasure from the back of a dealer's store room—and El Sueño is filled with great discoveries. But without hesitation, the most striking item I found for the house is the Clubhouse bar.

PRECEDING SPREAD: The elaborate coffered ceiling and mahogany millwork in the library evoke the spirit of a gentleman's reading room. The iron and brass detailing on the bookcase cabinet doors was inspired by a similar treatment in William Randolph Hearst's library at San Simeon. The 1930s coffee table is by noted French cabinetmaker Jules Leleu, the vintage leather chair is Swedish, and the pair of nineteenth-century silver chandeliers is German. OPPOSITE: This set of 1930s French nesting tables features scenes of Polynesian life, rendered in detailed marquetry.

Intended to resemble a Prohibition-era speakeasy, the Clubhouse is a handsome, walnut-paneled space designed for cocktails, cards, and cigars. With its gilded ceiling, smoking terrace, and expansive views of the outdoors, the room is a haven for the owner and anyone lucky enough to get a seat at the poker table. But for me, the room is all about the bar, a twelve-foot-long zinc-topped behemoth that was made in France in the 1920s and somehow ended up in Argentina, which is where I found it. After making the long journey north, the bar had to be hoisted up the side of a steep incline and lowered into its new home by an enormous crane. Victory indeed!

I walked away from this house after it was finished a decade ago, and was immensely pleased to be recently asked to elaborate and expand on what I started way back when. Originally built for a single man and his children, the house has evolved to reflect the lifestyle of the client and his new wife. It's been a wonderful experience to see the place through fresh eyes. Some elements have changed (the recently painted walls in the dining room truly bring that space to life), a number of things have been added, a few pieces have been reupholstered, and furniture has been moved around. The house takes it all in stride and is better for the refinements. Although the essential qualities of El Sueño remain, it's extremely gratifying to see the natural progression of a home maturing and finally coming into its own.

RIGHT: A palette of celadon and white was used for the kitchen, whereas a spirited green and a range of lavender and purple tones establish a more vibrant color scheme in the breakfast area. Classic McGuire rattan chairs are arrayed beneath a quirky, vintage painted-iron chandelier. FOLLOWING SPREAD: Spanish Prado rugs are a favorite of mine, but they can be difficult to find. The one we placed here dates to the 1920s and contributes to the vibrant color palette of this casual and sunny family room. The space leads to a covered loggia on one side, and the series of arch-topped French doors opens to a terrace that overlooks the pool on the other.

Originally from the estate of William Randolph Hearst, an elegant pair of hand-painted screens by Robert Crowder frames the Art Deco–inspired sleigh bed we designed for the master bedroom. The walls were hand-painted in a strié by Jean Horihata.

Her bathroom (above) conveys a decidedly feminine tone; his bathroom (opposite) is unapologetically masculine.

The Casita is a separate structure on the property that serves as the owner's private retreat. Along with an office, the building includes a room designated for the smoking and storage of cigars. The set of vintage leather wing chairs (above) is Swedish and surrounds a midcentury Danish table. The first piece purchased for the house was a desk (opposite) designed by Jules Leleu. It was made in the 1950s for the president of a French bank.

PICTURE PERFECT

For some of us, collecting art is a haphazard affair: an inherited painting, a poster from a favorite exhibition, a piece of sculpture purchased from an up-and-coming artist who also happens to be a friend. Then, of course, for some wildly rich hunter-gatherers, acquiring art is a contact sport. They travel to Basel or New York or London to see and be seen and can afford to buy whatever they want.

These clients are different. Their collection is extensive and marvelous, filled with pieces acquired over two generations by informed art lovers—passionate people committed to buying what they love and what they want to live with.

After raising a family in a traditional English Tudor–style house, my clients became aware that their collection not only had grown beyond the confines of their existing space but also wasn't being shown to particular advantage. They desperately needed blank walls—big, open walls and lots of them.

The only problem with having a collection so great and varied is having enough space to display it. So they set out to create a new house for themselves, which in turn would become a new home for their collection. Not a gallery or a museum in which they could live, but a proper house where the art could be truly appreciated.

Architect Marc Appleton was called in to design a classic residence that aesthetically fit the neighborhood, and had interior spaces that would answer the call for wall space.

Although the house is conventional from the outside (it references the time-honored white-brick American Georgian style), the interior detailing is crisp and minimally embellished. Traditional architectural elements—such as crown moldings, window casings, paneled doors, and baseboards—are painted white, allowing them to recede and making the works of art the true center of attention.

For me, the objective was quite clear: the backgrounds and furniture had to defer to the artwork in a respectful and cooperative manner. That didn't mean pieces couldn't be elegant or interesting or beautiful, just nothing that demanded too much attention. The art was the star, and the furnishings the supporting cast.

Japanese Edo-period bronze vases and an art-pottery bowl sit on top
of a contemporary steel-and-glass table from Blackman Cruz.

The objective was to create livable rooms where the clients could entertain family in an intimate setting, or host large fundraisers and gatherings that included visiting art dignitaries from around the world. Furnishings are spare, so every piece has to count. We established a palette of fairly neutral backgrounds that would appear throughout the house. The floors are bleached white oak, and most of the walls are in varying shades of white. (I tend to issue very complicated paint schedules containing scores of different hues, so this was a real challenge—I considered it a major victory when the clients agreed to sheathe the walls of the den in a taupe-colored linen.) Rugs and textiles soften any hard edges and provide texture. And in the spirit of modernism, only a few of the rooms have window treatments—a real blow for someone who loves festooning fabrics as much as I do.

One of our first purchases was a pair of Italian chairs for the living room. Dating to the 1940s and lending an air of *la dolce vita*, the chairs have an animated quality that adds an amusing counterpoint to the magnificent geometry of the Frank Stella painting.

At the opposite end of the room we placed two massive rosewood sofas with upholstery in a custom-woven fabric of linen and cotton. It's critical that all the furniture maintain a low profile so as not to interfere with the artwork in view, but these pieces surely hold their own against the enormous canvases of Morris Louis and Mark Bradford.

And although the artwork is clearly the jaw-dropping focal point of the room, for a decorative arts nerd like myself, the small table nestled between two Jules Leleu chairs is an exceptional jewel. Created by Jean-Michel Frank—considered by many to be one of the greatest interior and furniture designers of the twentieth century—the tortoiseshell-lacquer Parsons table was purchased directly from Frank by Frances Elkins, my personal interior design hero, in 1929. Top that piece with a charming miniature Alexander Calder stabile and there is cause for celebration.

Interwoven with contemporary furniture are wonderful examples from midcentury creators Milo Baughman and Willy Rizzo, as well as pieces from the 1980s. The 1970s console in the hallway is by Karl Springer, which much to my chagrin is now considered vintage furniture.

OPPOSITE: In the entry are a Jean Royère console, which dates to the 1940s and was purchased at auction, and a painting by Fernand Léger. FOLLOWING SPREAD: The height of the living room was dictated, in part, by the dimensions of the Morris Louis painting; miniature maquettes of the clients' works of art helped to determine placement. The rosewood sofas are joined by a pair of Jules Leleu wood-framed chairs from the 1930s. The red-lacquered orb on the coffee table is by Robert Kuo.

I introduced color strategically and selectively. Given that the collection rotates around the house (and on some occasions a piece might travel on loan to a museum exhibition), it would have been foolhardy to design a room around the colors in a specific painting. But I find that red can be a surprisingly neutral color—it goes with virtually everything—so I used a rich deep red for the Mario Bellini-designed Cab armchairs in the library and red leather for the lounge chairs in the den. For the moment these are happily situated within striking distance of paintings by Roy Lichtenstein, Willem de Kooning, and Martin Kippenberger, each of which incorporates variations of this marvelous hue.

The master bedroom is one of the few rooms in the house where you'll find curtains; here, they serve to make the large space feel cozy and layered. A silk carpet provides shimmer, and the palette of soft blues, lavenders, and taupes infuse the room with a feeling of tranquility and serenity—a counterpoint to the bold and decisive use of color in the Ellsworth Kelly and Cecily Brown paintings that dominate the room.

In most houses you would find windows flanking the dining room fireplace, but most houses don't have two shaped canvases by Kelly, hung on either side of a superb piece by Lichtenstein. Who needs windows when the view is this sublime? The room was designed to seat up to twenty-four guests who get to dine in a space that features works by some of the greatest artists of our time.

Throughout the process of decorating this house, I was always mindful of the relationships between furniture and artwork, owner and collection. It was a dream-come-true project for me—it's not often that one is asked to create a home for clients with a museum-worthy collection. And as someone whose fantasy is to own even just a single piece by one of the artists whose works hang on these walls, seeing my interiors as backgrounds for pieces by Richard Diebenkorn and David Hockney is absolute bliss. Who could ask for anything more?

OPPOSITE: An early Mark Bradford painting takes center stage between the living room's two seating areas. FOLLOWING SPREAD: A Frank Stella painting anchors the opposite end of the room. The slightly eccentric armchairs are 1940s Italian.

ABOVE: The curule-form stools are from New York antiques dealer Lee Calicchio. OPPOSITE: An Alexander Calder stabile rests on top of a Jean-Michel Frank tortoiseshell-lacquer table, which was purchased at auction. The piece was originally specified by noted interior decorator Frances Elkins for the Reed residence in Lake Forest, Illinois, which was completed in 1931. FOLLOWING SPREAD: A pair of Ellsworth Kelly paintings are a graphic counterpoint to a Roy Lichtenstein portrait. The walnut dining table was custom made to seat twenty-four guests, and its leaves are stored behind a purpose-built hidden panel.

ABOVE: The library's shelves accommodate an extensive collection of art books. OPPOSITE: A 1970s-era parchment-covered table and classic Cab armchairs in the library are seen at the end of the enfilade of rooms. FOLLOWING SPREAD: The interiors were designed to keep distracting patterns to a minimum; the only exception can be found in the antique Tabriz rug that was purchased for the den. The painting above the sofa on the right is by Julie Mehretu, and on the far wall is a piece by Willem de Kooning.

ABOVE: When I started this project, the client let me know her dream was to have a classic Eero Saarinen dining table and Tulip armchairs in her breakfast room; I was happy to oblige. A Yayoi Kusama flower sculpture in the garden beckons beyond. OPPOSITE: Neither distinctly traditional nor overtly contemporary, the kitchen strikes a balance between the two extremes. The light fixture over the island is vintage and was found in New York.

ABOVE: A diminutive sculpture by John Chamberlain and a Claes Oldenburg teacup are placed on a classic Karl Springer console from the 1970s. OPPOSITE: A bronze bench by noted French artisan Alexandre Logé sits beneath an early Alexander Calder mobile.

An Ellsworth Kelly
color-spectrum
painting provides a
graphic punch to a
space with a decidedly
subdued palette.

ARTS AND CRAFTSMANSHIP

When the property across the street from my client's house became available, there was cause for alarm.

Given Los Angeles's current affinity for houses on the monstrous end of the spectrum, the fear of a massive residence being erected directly opposite was not a paranoid fantasy. The existing structure would surely be razed by a new owner or developer, and with the specter of a fifteen-thousand-square-foot spec house on the horizon, there was only one option. With little hesitation, my client purchased the property.

But what do you do with a second home located less than twenty yards away from your primary residence? It's not quite a vacation destination. So the initial plan was to take down the existing place and build a playhouse for the client's young twins. Perhaps not the best idea given the land's value, but at least there wouldn't be an eyesore across the street.

But after a visit to Pasadena's landmark Gamble House, the playhouse morphed into a real house, and my client decided to follow the lead of early twentieth-century architects Greene and Greene and create an homage to the vernacular Arts and Crafts style.

The city's reputation for having a mishmash of building styles is well warranted. Drive down any street and you'll see Tudor next to French Regency, Tuscan villa next to Ranch, Spanish Revival next to American Colonial.

But early in the city's history, the Arts and Crafts style reigned, and this architectural genre accounted for a significant number of residential buildings in the teens and 1920s. During the nascent years of the city's growth, the shingled bungalow was ubiquitous. Some were kit houses available through Sears, Roebuck, and Company, but the Gamble House—which became the standard against which all other American Arts and Crafts houses are measured—took the style to the point of high art.

So when I was brought on board, the aesthetic mandate for the project would embrace the essence of the Arts and Crafts style, but with restraint and a dash of modernism. My mantra would be "Referential, not reverential."

As I do on any project with historical antecedents, I began by researching the work of Greene and Greene and other proponents of the movement in America and throughout the world. Craftsmanship was celebrated above all else as a rebuke to industrialization, which was considered dehumanizing. As a result, furniture was deceptively simple and, with visible joinery

OPPOSITE: On the entry console a lacquered Japanese plate and Edo-period bronze vases are grouped with an early twentieth-century vase from the Grueby Faience Company.
FOLLOWING SPREAD: A Milton Avery watercolor hangs on one of the entry's paneled oak walls. The Arts and Crafts chair is by the Charles P. Limbert Furniture Company, the vintage lantern is French, and the bronze lamps are by Danish metalworker Just Andersen.

highlighted as evidence of the craftsman's artistry, mortise-and-tenon construction became a hallmark of pieces made during that era.

Although the major player in the American Arts and Crafts movement was Gustav Stickley, I was reluctant to fill the house with his pieces. Perhaps it was an over-reaction to the Arts and Crafts trend that exploded in the mid-1980s, but I felt collecting the more predictable representations of this style of furniture would render the interiors a bit bland. (Barbra Streisand would ultimately set an auction record—$363,000—for a Stickley sideboard, a purchase often cited as the death knell that sent the market for this type of furniture into a downward spiral.)

Given that the house would be relatively small, everything we selected or made had to convey the spirit of the movement, but without the heft of these often ponderous pieces. I found a pair of hand-carved chairs and a chunky console made in the 1920s by Swedish furniture designer Axel Einar Hjorth and combined them with Morris chairs from France (named for William Morris, the father of English Arts and Crafts). We added Japanese lanterns and French stools, a Chinese coffee table, an English standing lamp, and American art pottery. This veritable United Nations of artisans wouldn't have been found in a traditional Craftsman bungalow, but a harmonious sensibility binds these disparate objects together.

Early in the project I came across a vintage hand-embroidered tablecloth that sadly was well beyond repair, but the cross-stitch detail in a corner became the inspiration for the custom area rug we made for the den. The Craftsman motif is clearly evident, but the exaggerated scale is a bit unexpected; the rug provides pattern and a jolt of color in the otherwise patternless space.

One of my great passions is shopping for antique and vintage lighting, and this project gave me the perfect opportunity to fill a house with exceptional examples of period fixtures. Favorites include a goatskin-and-hammered-copper hanging light in the den and a spectacular pair of lanterns, attributed to Frank Lloyd Wright, over the dining table. As phenomenal as these fixtures are, the one I most adore is a bronze lantern designed by the Dutch-born architect Alexander Kropholler that hangs serenely in the stairwell—a serendipitous discovery I made while walking down the rue de Lille in Paris on a Sunday afternoon.

Above all, the house had to be comfortable and inviting, but fully upholstered furniture was not standard issue in residences decorated in the Arts and Crafts style.

The design for the den's area rug was inspired by a small fragment of an Arts and Crafts textile—I modified the graphic motifs and enlarged the scale to create a more contemporary interpretation. The room features a mix of Arts and Crafts furniture from England, China, and France along with a magnificent landscape by David Hockney.

ABOVE: The den's ceiling fixture—made of goatskin and hammered copper—is French and dates to circa 1910. OPPOSITE: I collected period Arts and Crafts pottery during the course of the project and placed the pieces throughout the house—here, atop a circa-1915 English oak-and-leather table. FOLLOWING SPREAD: The furnishings in the living room—representing a wide range of influences, countries, and artisans—include a console table and chairs by noted Swedish designer Axel Einar Hjorth, a pair of stools by French furniture maker Charles Dudouyt, Japanese bronze-and-paper lanterns, a Morris chair from France, an English copper standing lamp, American art pottery, and a custom bronze-and-rift-oak coffee table with faux-bamboo legs.

ABOVE: Hammered-copper Arts and Crafts accessories on an English copper tray table in the living room. The hand-carved chair is by Axel Einar Hjorth. OPPOSITE: I loved shopping for Arts and Crafts accessories for this house. On the living room coffee table I grouped these exquisite vases, which were purchased at various shops and at auction.

OPPOSITE: We couldn't find an appropriate dining table large enough to seat twenty, so we designed this one of rift oak. The chairs were also custom made and are based on a classic style by Danish designer Kaare Klint. ABOVE: The pair of bronze-and-glass lanterns is attributed to Frank Lloyd Wright.

(Most of the sofas and settees designed by Stickley feature wood frames with firm seat cushions—not all that cozy by my standards.) So I created pieces that conform to more contemporary tastes for lounging and leisure. Chairs are deep and soft, and although we incorporated a rift-oak base (the preferred wood for American Arts and Crafts furniture), our sectional couldn't be more of-the-moment in terms of upholstered seating.

For a house this size it's rare to see separate powder rooms for men and women, but that's what my client wanted. How lucky for me, because I'd come across an exuberant pair of Tramp Art mirrors and now had a perfect excuse to use them both. I have a source in Los Angeles for authentic vintage plumbing and found two period sinks—each in perfect condition. We lined the upper portion of the men's room with period wallpaper—unused stock from the 1920s—and I reproduced the sconces from pairs that graced the Gamble House. (If you could even find a pair of original Greene and Greene sconces, they'd cost a small fortune.) I discovered—and fell in love with—a woodblock print in a book. I had Jean Horihata, a decorative artist I've worked with for decades, enlarge the scale of the print and hand paint a mural for the women's powder room. This room lacks a window, so when you open the door you're completely transported to the light-filled lakeside bower Jean created.

The master bedroom—lined in board-and-batten wainscoting and softened by a silk carpet and embroidered window treatments—is a play between past and present. A painting by Ed Ruscha hangs above a rift-oak-and-leather bed we designed and had made with traditional joinery techniques. A magnificent chest by German architect Otto Schulz dates to 1918 but feels modern given the geometric rhythm of its doors and drawers. It stands just opposite a pair of contemporary cloisonné tabourets by noted furniture artisan Robert Kuo.

This house was designed as a modernist homage to Greene and Greene, with elaborate millwork, classic "cloud lift" detailing on the doors and cabinetry, and simple yet stylized architectural flourishes evocative of the masters' work. We found someone who made hand-blown milk glass for the living room skylight and incorporated old-fashioned materials like linoleum for the kitchen floors and laundry room counters. And although the house is redolent with Arts and Crafts embellishments, we decided early on to eschew anything that might feel forced or ersatz. The result is a house that doesn't pretend to be from another time—it acknowledges the past while being strongly grounded in the sensibilities of today.

OPPOSITE: The embroidery pattern on the linen curtain panel in the men's powder room is based on a detail we discovered on an Arts and Crafts chair. The hand-printed wallpaper is vintage unused stock from the early 1920s. PAGES 168 AND 169: Distinctly different, but complementary, the men's and women's powder rooms each feature one of a pair of superb Tramp Art mirrors and vintage porcelain sinks from circa 1900. Both pairs of custom sconces are based on ones originally designed by noted architects Greene and Greene. The walls of the women's room were painted by Jean Horihata, a frequent collaborator.

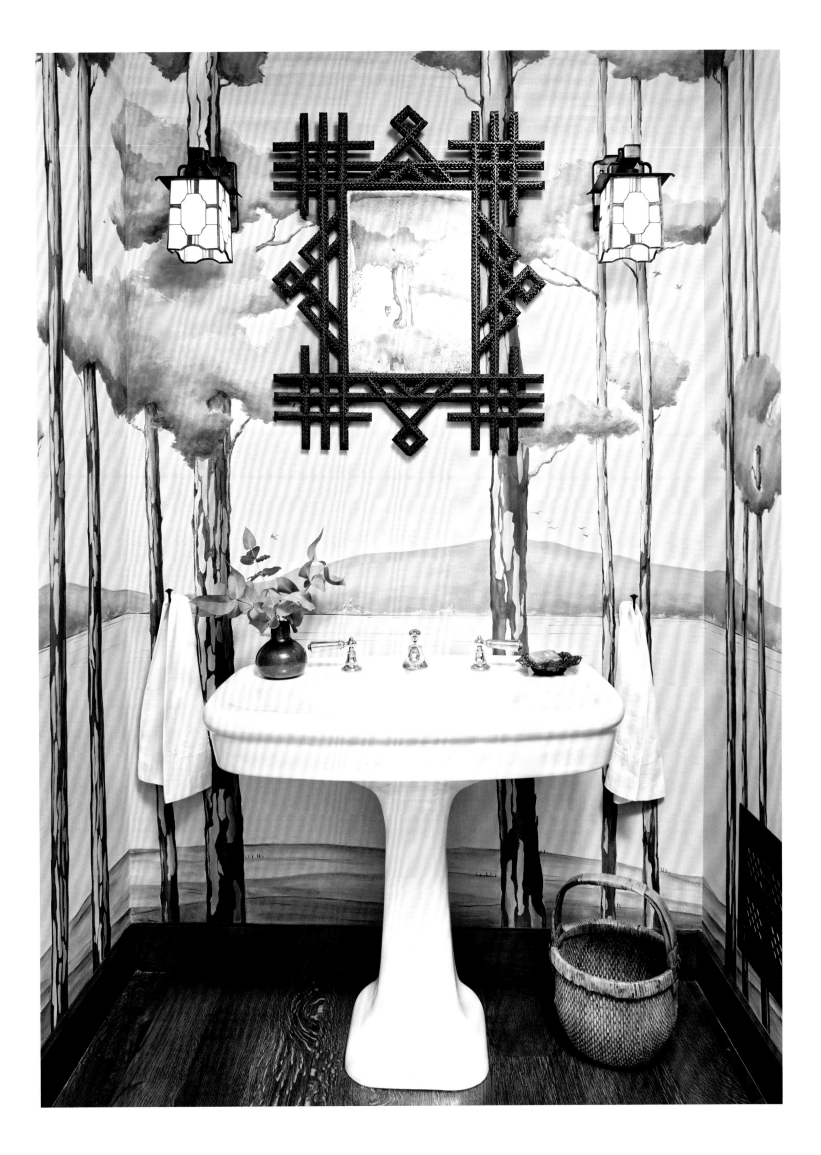

ABOVE: I love using wicker, and these chairs are a perfect complement to the classic vintage rift-oak table that we found for the kitchen's breakfast area. OPPOSITE: The kitchen is clearly modern, but the detailing on the cabinetry alludes to the house's Arts and Crafts spirit. The floor is linoleum (an old-fashioned material that I adore), which is set in a classic checkerboard pattern.

OPPOSITE: Two of my favorite finds are in the stairwell. The lantern is by Dutch architect Alexander Kropholler, and the chair is by Charles Rohlfs, a noted designer of the Arts and Crafts period. Most of Rohlfs's pieces are far more eccentric than this rather staid hall chair. PAGE 174: The custom chairs and ottoman ground the seating area at the far end of the master bedroom. The fireplace surround is made of hand-hammered copper, and the desk is Danish from the 1920s. PAGE 175: An impressive chest from 1918 by German architect Otto Schulz is perhaps the most important piece I purchased for the house.

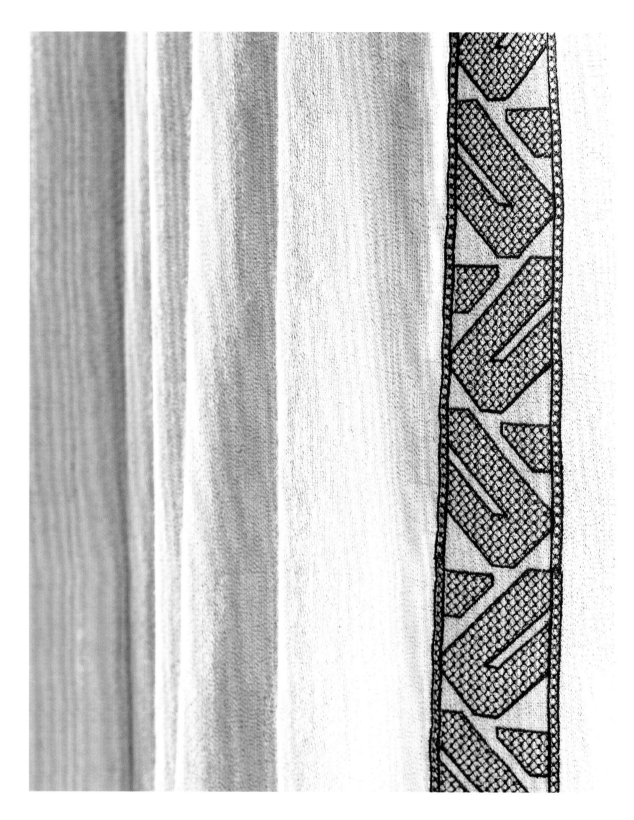

ABOVE: Drapery panels in the master bedroom were embroidered with a pattern that, though not specifically Arts and Crafts in origin, feels appropriate to the period. OPPOSITE: We incorporated traditional Arts and Crafts joinery techniques into this custom rift-oak-and-leather bed. The glazed ceramic lamps are the work of Christopher Dresser, an English designer of the nineteenth-century Aesthetic movement. The painting above the bed is by Ed Ruscha. PAGE 178: Her bathroom features classic Chinese detailing on the cabinetry, a nod to the significant influence of Asian design on the work of Greene and Greene. The nickel-plated sconces, ceiling fixture, and stool were all custom made for the room. PAGE 179: In contrast, his bathroom is fully paneled with a planked ceiling that evokes a ship's hull. The space is distinguished by dark bronze fittings and Arts and Crafts sconces from circa 1905.

MODERNE HISTORY

If you've read or heard anything about the significant houses of Los Angeles, then you might know something about the Cedric Gibbons / Dolores del Rio house, a Streamline Moderne masterpiece built in 1930. I was certainly familiar with the residence, but only through images—I'd yet to see it in person. So it was a thrill when my clients invited me to join them on a tour of the property, as it was for sale and they were in the mood to buy.

That's where the story starts. But first, a little background about Gibbons and his remarkable work.

Cedric Gibbons is undoubtedly the most famous art director in Hollywood history. He not only is credited with the sets for more than fifteen hundred films (among them *The Wizard of Oz*) at Metro-Goldwyn-Mayer Studios (MGM), where he reigned for almost four decades, but also was nominated for the Academy Award thirty-seven times and won eleven Oscars, a statuette of his own design.

Gibbons traveled to Paris in 1925 to attend the influential Exposition des Arts Decoratifs, which gave birth to the now familiar term *Art Deco*. He returned to MGM, where his set designs reflected some of the architectural and decorative motifs that were prevalent at the exposition. He designed grandly scaled interiors with such elements as geometric flourishes, highly polished black floors, and walls and ceilings with stepped detailing. (Prior to Gibbons, most film sets were merely painted backdrops—he insisted on creating fully realized, three-dimensional spaces.)

In the late 1920s, Gibbons decided to design a house of his own, a residence he would share with his new bride, the breathtakingly beautiful Mexican-born actress Dolores del Rio. He engaged a practicing architect to facilitate the plans, but every last feature of the house refers to Gibbons's fabulous film sets, which reflect the influence of the exhibition on him.

This was a house built for entertaining: tennis competitions with famous Hollywood stars and extravagantly catered pool parties. On any one of the seven built-in banquettes, conversations often ended in canoodling. Gibbons and del Rio were an incredibly glamorous couple and lived a similarly glamorous life.

But the marriage didn't last, and the house was sold. And sold again. And again. In all, there have been nine owners since the day Gibbons moved out. Astonishingly enough, the house underwent very few changes over the years. The kitchen had been updated, and the pool house rebuilt; there were some minor additional alterations, but otherwise the structure reflected its creator's unique artistic vision—right down to the five-thousand-two-hundred square feet of black linoleum flooring.

The entrance to the Cedric Gibbons / Dolores del Rio house has remained unchanged since the house was completed in 1930. (That includes the nearly three-hundred-pound stainless-steel door.)

Of course this didn't mean there weren't innumerable restorative measures that needed to be taken. In order to make the house suitable for my clients, significant changes were required. Specifically, the master bedroom, closet, and bathroom needed to be enlarged.

Initially I had grave reservations about transforming the existing structure and wasn't convinced an addition could be seamlessly integrated. The house was proportionally perfect and architecturally important, and I didn't want to be the one with blood on my hands, should the remodeling project destroy the integrity of this iconic place. So I called out for help, asking my friend and frequent collaborator Kevin A. Clark to come by and take a look.

ABOVE: The stunning Mexican-born actress Dolores del Rio sitting on the living room stairs.
OPPOSITE: The same dramatic stainless-steel balustrade today. The steps are terrazzo.
FOLLOWING SPREAD: One of the original banquettes flanking the staircase. Gibbons created seven of these built-in divans for the living room and second-floor salon.

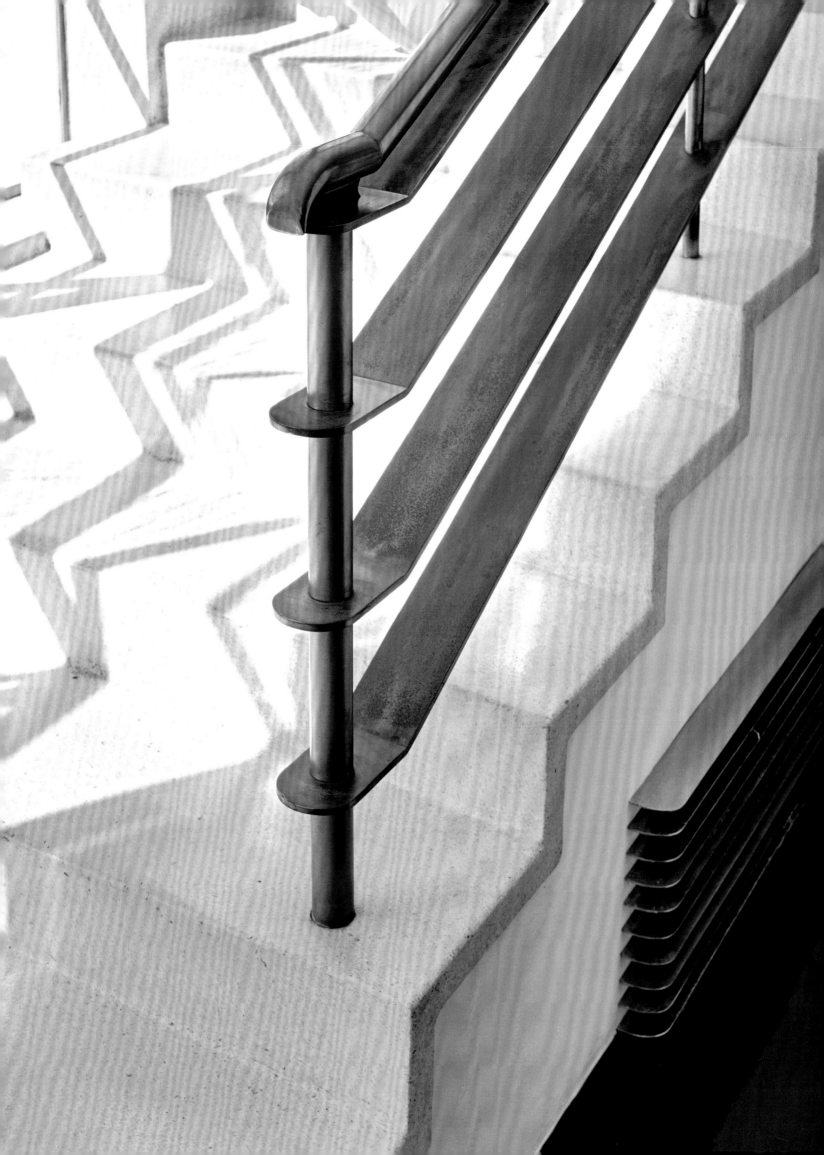

PRECEDING PAGES: Art Deco interiors are often thought of as being monochromatic, which is merely because the images we associate with the era were photographed in black and white. I opted for a richly hued palette that's meant to convey a 1930s sensibility. Mirrors—like the one over the banquette—are used in many of the rooms, ostensibly as a tribute to del Rio's beauty. ABOVE: The Swedish Rya rug dates to the 1950s, but the geometric motif feels very much of the Art Deco period. OPPOSITE: The hammered-copper vessel is from the 1930s.

ABOVE: The dining room's area rug was designed by Émile Gaudissart in 1925 and was the very first thing we purchased. It set the tone for the colors we would ultimately use throughout the house. OPPOSITE: The parchment (goatskin), mahogany, and bronze table is by Mexican architect and designer Arturo Pani. Two of the chairs are by Jules Leleu and date to the 1930s. The remaining ten chairs were reproduced almost exactly—a couple of inches were added to the width and depth to accommodate the proportions of modern-day diners. PAGES 192 AND 193: The powder room's silver-leafed walls were hand painted by decorative artist Jean Horihata. The design of the 1930s chest echoes the stepped architectural detailing that's prevalent in the house.

ABOVE: Gibbons and del Rio, sitting on the same banquette almost ninety years before the photographs for this book were taken. OPPOSITE: The 1940s chairs are French, and the vintage table is by Italian designer Guglielmo Ulrich. FOLLOWING SPREAD: A room of cinematic proportions, the second-floor salon is a masterstroke of Streamline Moderne architecture. With its stepped detailing, polished linoleum floors, and multiple seating areas, it is elegant, glamorous, sophisticated, transportive—and just a little louche. When you enter this room, it's like traveling back in time.

It didn't take Kevin long to sketch an absolutely inspired solution, and thus the project began in earnest. We added a master wing on the second floor with a completely new bathroom and his-and-hers closets. Beneath that we built a redesigned library, a sun room with retracting steel-and-glass doors, and a new guest bathroom. In a musty corner of the basement, we carved out a room for wine storage. Adjacent to the pool, Kevin created entirely new guest quarters in what had been a moldy mess above the garage. All that was left was the restoration of the walls in the existing tennis pavilion—the original linoleum panels had long since deteriorated. And every inch of the of black linoleum flooring would have to be removed and replaced with matching material, polished to a high mirror gloss that would replicate the original.

So how does one start to design the interiors of a landmark 1930s house? For me, the process began with extensive research into the period: its architectural styles and influences; its great designers; the textiles, furniture, and lighting; and the artists and artisans whose work reflected the dominant aesthetic. We compiled a massive dossier of images that helped define our vision, inform the process, and convey our intentions.

From the start we determined that our palette would embrace and celebrate colors suggestive of the Jazz Age. Although people tend to think of Art Deco style in terms of black and white, that's mainly because the images indelibly etched into our collective consciousness are from old black-and-white photos. In truth, it was an era of mauve, teal, puce, emerald green, ruby red, pale lavender, buttery yellow, and soft orange, and we incorporated all of these into our scheme.

Gibbons and del Rio pose in front of the salon's asymmetric fireplace, circa 1930.

198

Because the interior architecture of the house is so crisp—with soft white walls and those blackest-of-black floors—we wanted to counter the austerity with luxurious textures. So we pulled together hundreds of fabric samples and arranged them in groupings that would ultimately determine the feel of each room. There were linen velvets, cotton velvets, cut velvets, and silk velvets in varying shades. We added lustrous silks and satins of the type that might have been worn by Jean Harlow. We included hand-woven textiles to balance the shiny ones (this is a family house after all) and threw in quite a number of Fortuny fabrics, which are still made on a small island in Venice.

Given the severity of the black linoleum flooring, finding the right area rug for each room was critical. Our very first purchase was a vintage carpet created in Paris in 1925 (the year of the exposition) and designed by Émile Gaudissart. I discovered it in New York and had it shipped to Los Angeles to see how it looked in the space. From the moment we unrolled it on the dusty floor (the house was in construction and completely torn apart), we knew it was the one. There are thousands of beautiful rugs in the world, but this one spoke to the house and the period, and it contained virtually every color we ultimately decided to use.

Although that carpet dates to around the time the house was conceived, there was no attempt to restrict ourselves to rugs and furniture from a prescribed period. The fabulous Swedish Rya carpet that dominates the downstairs living room is from the 1950s, yet its geometric flourish in the center feels very suggestive of the 1930s, and the pair of shaggy mohair area rugs in the upper-level salon was custom made for the house. They're completely modern but exude a luxe, calm, and voluptuous air that's perfect for the space.

My clients had been living in a Mediterranean-style house, so virtually none of their furniture would be appropriate for Gibbons's style-specific structure. (We ultimately used only one thing from their previous residence—a pair of French leather club chairs from the 1930s landed in the library.) Everything else would be purchased specially for this home.

Many of the distinctive features designed by Gibbons were thankfully still intact. There was a built-in buffet as well as storage cabinets in the dining room, and the salon had bookcases on three walls. Multiple banquettes defined the seating areas on both floors, but unfortunately they were unsuitably deep. My theory is that they were intended for sprawling—not sitting upright. To allow for polite conversation, we added backs to each one to minimize the overall depth. That said, they're still deep enough for lolling about, should one be so inclined.

We wanted a showstopping piece for the center of the second-floor salon and discovered a fabulous sycamore-and-ebony table dating to 1932 and designed by Dominique, the famous Parisian decorating firm. What I love about the furniture we found for this project is the sheer range of periods, countries, and artisans. The dining table of parchment (goatskin), mahogany, and bronze is by the noted Mexican architect Arturo Pani, and dates to the late 1950s. Pani also designed the living room's coffee table and the lamps in the master bedroom. The salon's multiple coffee tables are Austrian, French, and Italian, and there are lounge chairs from 1915 and the

ABOVE AND OPPOSITE: A corner of the salon features a pair of Danish chairs from the 1930s covered in silk velvet.

The master bathroom was completely remodeled but retains the spirit of Gibbons's design—this is a theatrical space where black marble and mirror reign supreme. The floor is made of shards of black marble, and the ceiling fixture is Lalique, designed by Leleu. The foot pedals (above)—one for hot, one for cold—control the master bathroom sink faucet and are original to the house. We saved and reused the little nickel stars that are scattered on the mirrors—perhaps they were originally meant as a reference to del Rio's star status?

1930s that are Swedish and Danish, respectively. We came across a stunning pair of dining chairs by the French master Jules Leleu and had another ten made to replicate the originals, but with a slight adjustment for modern proportions. (Dining chairs from earlier eras tend to be a bit small in scale for contemporary physiques.)

When we set out to create a new master bathroom, our goal was to retain not only the original glamour but also the existing sink stands and little nickel stars that were scattered about the walls. This space is now a tour de force of black marble, black lacquer, and mirror. Shards of black marble create a mosaic on the floor, and the ceiling is crowned by a vintage Lalique globe, also designed by Leleu. Most surprisingly, the clients insisted on keeping the existing controls for the sink faucet's hot and cold water, which are located on the floor and operated by foot pedals. (Look, Ma, no hands!)

The very last piece we found—long after we'd finished the project—is a fabulous plaster bas-relief of a mermaid, designed by a Belgian artist and cast in the early 1930s. Its poundage is so substantial that in order to mount it to the far end of the sun room, the wall had to be opened up and a steel plate installed to support the weight. She now beams beatifically over a set of custom stick wicker furniture, seemingly unaware that the ocean is only a mile or so to the west.

It was a formidable challenge to respect and honor this architecturally significant residence while simultaneously reworking it as a family home some ninety years after its creation. I, for one, think period rooms are for museums, and decorating in a specific genre now feels terribly out of date. Thus, there was never an attempt to re-create interiors that strictly adhered to a 1930s aesthetic, but we clearly set out to embrace the general feeling, style, and ambiance of that era. By incorporating all these seemingly disparate elements, from various countries, periods, and artists, we were able to establish a unique and personal vision for this house and the people who live there.

Los Angeles has been distressingly unconcerned with its architectural heritage, and it seems that every day another important house, landmark, or period structure is reduced to a pile of rubble. It might be a small Arts and Crafts bungalow that's demolished in order to build a lot-line-to-lot-line contemporary box or a midcentury Googie-style coffee shop torn down to erect another pointless mini mall. So it's a rare thing to be granted the opportunity to save and restore an authentic jewel box, one that dates to the early part of the twentieth century (ancient by Los Angeles standards).

How lovely that this family now holds tennis matches and charity events on the court, throws pool parties and dinners, and uses and enjoys every space on the property. And how gratifying it is that these clients are committed preservationists, willing to save this house and do whatever it took to ensure its future. In a town that's rarely been concerned with protecting and preserving its past, the Gibbons / del Rio house continues to be a true star.

A new addition under the expanded master wing, the sun room features custom rattan furniture based on classic styles from the 1930s. The steel-and-glass doors retract into the side walls so the room can open to the garden. The tennis pavilion can be seen in the background.

RIGHT: In the tennis pavilion we designed a geometric pattern of colored plaster with stainless-steel inlay to approximate the look of the original linoleum walls, which had long since deteriorated. The seating was custom made in the spirit of Warren McArthur, whose tubular aluminum furniture was much in vogue in the 1930s. Our custom pieces join a few of McArthur's originals, which are placed throughout the property. PAGES 208 AND 209: The circa-1930s light fixture is one we installed, but the stylized railing that leads to the tennis seating area was extant. The umpire chair required extensive repair, but it's the same chair that del Rio is famously pictured sitting in with her beloved dog. PAGES 210-11: The rear elevation of the iconic Gibbons / del Rio house. The addition (far right) has been seamlessly integrated into Gibbons's Streamline Moderne masterpiece.

HOME ON THE RANGE

Every student of American history learns that when Meriwether Lewis and William Clark set out to map the western United States in 1804 and 1805, they camped near Three Forks, Montana, where the Jefferson, Gallatin, and Madison rivers converge to form the mighty Missouri. What the textbooks fail to mention, however, is that the intrepid explorers almost certainly spent time on the property acquired more than two hundred years later by my clients, who chose to build a campsite that is far more exalted than that of Lewis and Clark.

With spring-fed creeks, verdant pastures, cool ponds, and exceptional vistas that enhance glorious sunsets, this little corner of Montana now provides sheer summer bliss for a family of four, a few dogs, quite a number of horses, and those fortunate enough to receive an invitation to the ranch.

For years after acquiring the property, the family crowded together in a tiny old log cabin. Cramped but cozy, it enabled them to spend time forging a deeper understanding of the type of house they ultimately wanted to build on this special plot of land.

The question of where to situate the house was solved by my client, who came to realize that rather than build on the highest point of the property, the structure should be sited lower and near one of the creeks so the family could hear the sound of water.

Enter architect David Lake of highly respected Lake|Flato Architects, who conceived a deceptively simple structure close to the ground and nestled into a hillside. Bracketed by porches, the main building is essentially a modernist lodge and is divided into areas for living, cooking, and dining. The bedroom wing is tucked around the corner, accessed by a covered walkway and crowned with a sod roof.

Early in the project, David and I established a palette of basic building materials that would set a thematic consistency and require minimal maintenance. The roof is Cor-Ten steel, the ceilings and walls are a combination of stained Douglas fir and reclaimed wood, the floors are polished concrete, and the structural walls are fashioned from board-form concrete with the inherent knots, seams, and aberrations celebrated rather than concealed.

We took an egalitarian approach to the sleeping quarters—most are about the same size—small by some measures, but days are long here in the summer and virtually all one's time is spent outside. The bathrooms are nearly identical, with darkened steel counters, horizontal paneling of Douglas fir, and shower floors fashioned from small river stones. Architecturally and decoratively, the imperative was to keep it simple.

The mandate for the interiors was clear from the start: nothing fragile, precious, or fussy, no tabletops that might require coasters. The furniture, rugs, and fabrics were expected to be tough enough to accommodate dogs, kids, and muddy boots.

A vintage macramé wall hanging against board-form concrete walls

Most Montana homesteads tend toward the traditional in terms of furnishings, but this is not a typical Montana home. Rustic Modern is the term I adopted for the interiors, and from the beginning it was clear we would forge a unique and decidedly nontraditional approach to the design. We sought to create an environment that's warm and welcoming, understated yet sophisticated. We incorporated colors and materials that defer to the authentic character of the place without adhering to the familiar Western plaid-and-antlers design trope.

When I start a new project, the path ahead is not always apparent or predetermined. My approach is more evolutionary, and I welcome the serendipitous find that might ultimately light the way. Often a single item establishes the aesthetic direction. That was undoubtedly the case here.

Two hulking black-leather-and-rosewood chairs designed by Brazilian architect and furniture artisan Sergio Rodrigues were the first purchase. A somewhat unorthodox choice, these humongous loungers are quirky, gutsy, and insanely comfortable. With a decidedly 1970s vibe, they determined the tone for the entire house. These may be the first Rodrigues chairs to make their way to this part of the American West, but I think cowboys would approve.

We set about selecting the rest of the furnishings with the intention of mixing, not matching. Various styles, periods, and influences are represented throughout. Verner Panton's elliptical leather rockers are positioned to take advantage of the views, and the glazing on the hilariously oversized 1960s-era ceramic lamps mimics the browns, greens, and blues in the surrounding landscape. An almost matched set of Hans Wegner leather armchairs surrounds a dining table I designed of claro walnut with a bronze base. A mammoth metal armature overhead supports two vintage Lightolier fixtures that we found and had painted to match the steel trusses and beams that support the roof.

The custom flat-weave rug that anchors the living room was inspired by classic Navajo patterns, which I find to be surprisingly contemporary. In the primarily black-and-white rug, I scattered shots of blue and added a single band of red at the edge, just because I wanted to.

One of our most extraordinary finds became the centerpiece of the living room, a monumental (and massively heavy) slice of a tree trunk that serves as the coffee table. Brazilian in origin, it joins a Rodrigues-designed rosewood sofa with cushions of pale leather and pillows of locally sourced fur. (Added note: Beavers are incredibly damaging to the creeks on the ranch and are routinely trapped. Although PETA supporters would be horrified by the beaver pillows and blanket we made from their pelts for the master bedroom, the fish who live in those creeks are extremely grateful.)

OPPOSITE: A view of the David Lake–designed house from across the spring-fed swimming hole. FOLLOWING SPREAD: A vintage Sergio Rodrigues bench is positioned beneath antique English train racks in the entry. A Verner Panton rocker can be seen in the distance. PAGES 218-19: The house is essentially a single space divided into areas for living, cooking, and dining, with a screened-in porch at the far end. The retaining walls are board-form concrete, and the interior walls are a combination of reclaimed wood and Douglas fir.

PAGE 220: A fossilized horn—found on the property—rests on the ancient wood slab that serves as the top of the coffee table in the living area. PAGE 221: An assemblage of thousands of wooden pieces, installed on a wall of the dining area, is by an unknown artist and was probably made in the 1970s. RIGHT: Vintage Hans Wegner chairs surround a custom table of claro walnut and bronze. The steel truss system overhead is as elegant as it is structural.

ABOVE AND OPPOSITE: The goal for the project's palette and materials was to keep it simple, so we used blackened steel in the kitchen—for the walls, stove hood, and island counter. PAGES 226 AND 227: A sunny corner of the screened-in porch is a coveted spot for an intimate lunch. The woven rope chairs are French from the 1940s.

Throughout the house, we softened spaces by incorporating myriad textures in the rugs and fabrics. So while leather prevails (there is hardly a more durable material), performance fabrics mix with hair on hide, curly lamb sidles up to shearling, and coarsely woven silk is combined with blankets of fuzzy wool.

It's not uncommon for the ranch to host lunches for twenty and dinners for twice that number, and fancy china was out of the question. We designed a livestock brand and had it emblazoned on dinnerware of the type used in diners and embroidered the logo on napkins, placemats, and aprons. I found all manner and sizes of carved wooden bowls—some for a song and others quite collectible—for use as decorative elements as well as for serving chips. A favorite pastime of mine is hunting for vintage, one-of-a-kind handmade ceramic vases, plates, and vessels, which I placed on living room and bedroom tables as well as bathroom counters. The smallest one is barely the size of a ping-pong ball, yet it's a focal point in a grouping I positioned next to the giant lamp in the living room.

On the Sunset Porch, where cocktails and conversation converge before dinner, I designed lounge chairs custom made for the ranch out of reclaimed barn wood, a nod to the humble and stalwart traditions of Montana.

At the opposite end of the building is a screened-in porch, retrofitted with sliding glass doors a year or so after the house was completed. Although the furniture we bought and made for this room was intended to withstand the harsh environmental conditions of blisteringly hot summers and witheringly cold winters, no one could have anticipated that a snowstorm was capable of forcing its way through the screens, resulting in snowdrifts up to five feet deep, blanketing the porch's interiors and completely burying the custom rift-oak chairs and sofas. I'm eternally grateful that the vintage French rope chairs that surround the dining table are now snowflake free.

Summers bring the ranch alive, and my clients entertain a seemingly endless stream of friends and family who ride, bike, hike, swim, and fish. Target practice using the empty wine bottles from the previous night's dinner is a favorite sport. I'm a surprisingly good shot, although for me, the idea of a perfect day is doing nothing more strenuous than finding the ideal place to sit and read.

I had never been to Montana before I started this project. And although I'd certainly heard it referred to as Big Sky Country, it was nothing more than a slogan until I came under the region's spell. Now I appreciate why Lewis and Clark chose to tarry here, and I feel incredibly lucky to have helped make a home for my clients in the very same place.

OPPOSITE: The furniture surrounding the fireplace on the screened-in porch is a combination of custom and vintage. The sofa and chairs were made for the room, but the stools are 1960s Italian. The effort of six men was required to carry in the solid-stone top for the iron coffee table base. PAGES 230 AND 231: A vintage Arne Norell leather sling chair and a Jorge Zalszupin stump table sit opposite the custom woven-leather-and-rift-oak bed in the master bedroom. PAGES 232-33: Custom lounge chairs fabricated from reclaimed barn wood provide the perfect perch for cocktails on the Sunset Porch.

ITALIAN SPLENDOR

When the call came, construction was well underway—the project had been in development for nearly five years, and building had started two years before I was contacted.

Progress with a previous designer had stalled. The clients wanted the interiors to proceed in a different direction and chose me to chart the new course. (It's not unheard of for clients to change horses in midstream, and I'm grateful to have been the beneficiary here.)

The house was rising on the site of the owners' previous residence, a Tudor-style pile that had been a family retreat since the 1970s. Although filled with memories, it wasn't a great house, and repeated attempts to redesign and remodel it had proved difficult at the least, and unsatisfactory at best. Tearing it down was the only logical conclusion.

The issue of the style for the new house was considered by all five members of the family. A consensus was required (presumably every vote carried equal weight, but I have a theory about the identity of the decider in this tight-knit group). Ultimately, they determined that the residence should be in the manner of an Italian villa built around an interior courtyard fashioned as a columned cloister with a central fountain.

Los Angeles teems with faux-Italianate residences, scattered throughout its most sought-after neighborhoods. These homes borrow liberally from the architectural dictionary, and most are a hodgepodge of pseudo-Mediterranean gestures. Broadly interpreted, this means anything containing an arched door or a concrete balustrade.

Fortunately, my clients were extremely familiar with significant examples of Italian architecture, and they were determined to create a residence that was graciously proportioned, quietly elegant, and suitable to the site.

This was never going to be a house that could be described as Tuscan Modern. The imperative was to create a beautiful, welcoming place for immediate and extended family, and with that goal in mind, the clients engaged the New York–based architectural firm Ferguson and Shamamian.

Mark Ferguson and project architect Scott Sottile crafted a plan that provided plenty of bedrooms for family members and relatives along with areas that suited the family's desire to cook, eat, and entertain together. Mark and Scott created rooms for living, not just for show. They established a hierarchy of public and private spaces, relocated the pool, and designed a pavilion on the far side of the property that's essentially a living room with a spectacular view of the rear facade. There are spots for outdoor lounging and alfresco dining, and there's a covered loggia where you can sit and contemplate the garden and its towering sycamore trees.

What might appear to be thousands of stars in the galaxy are actually tiny pieces of eggshell set in to the top of a 1930s black-lacquered tray table in the living room.

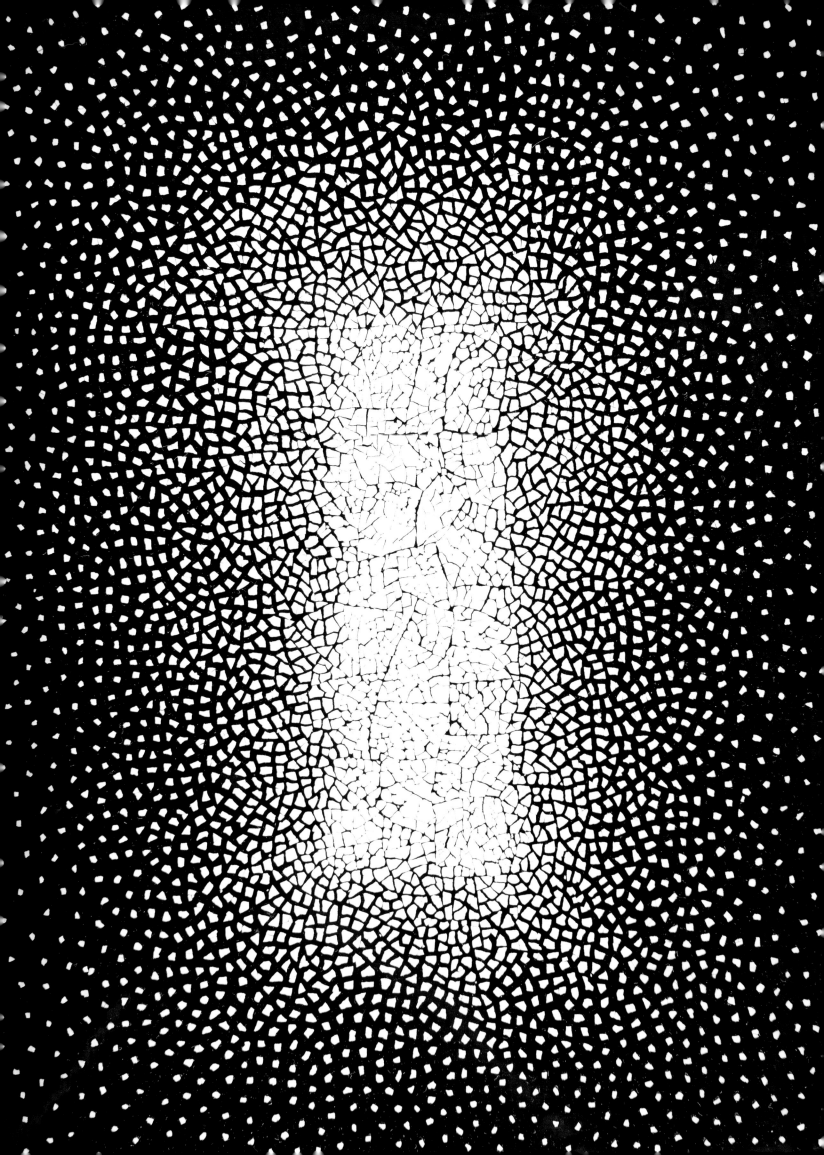

After joining the team, I set out to establish a new approach to the interior design. My firm and I created a dossier of imagery to express our ideas for the house, and we were relieved (and delighted) to discover that our clients were in complete accord.

This is a classic house in terms of its architectural form, but my goal was to fill it with pieces culled from a wide variety of sources. I didn't want to be forced to choose between what might be considered strictly traditional or resolutely modern, nor was I aiming my arrow to hit the transitional bull's-eye. In the images that served as inspiration, a beautiful balance of objects and elements represented various eras and influences. I didn't want the interiors to be pigeonholed as one thing or another.

I initially focused on decisions that had a direct impact on the construction schedule, thus stone and tile specifications, wall and floor finishes, and material selections became the first priority. Every family member had their own ideas about color and pattern, so I worked to create rooms for each that responded to their individual input. One daughter selected soft shades of pale pink and taupe marble for her bathroom, and her sister gravitated toward a bold combination of black-and-white geometric patterned floors with shockingly bright teal walls.

The master bathrooms and dressing rooms are worlds unto themselves and capture the essence of yin and yang. Dark and handsome might best describe his side of the master suite, while hers is unapologetically pretty and feminine. Delicate birds and foliage grace the hand-painted Chinese tea paper in her bathroom, which is dressed in creamy white and celadon-colored marble.

Given the scale of some of the rooms, I determined early on to incorporate all manner of wall treatments to provide warmth and texture throughout the house. Wood paneling, grass-cloth wall covering, lime-wash paint, Venetian plaster, paper-backed silk, hand-combed plaster, hand-painted Chinese wallpaper, and walls with custom-painted decorative motifs ended up working to marvelous effect. Faux-stone blocks line the stairwell walls en route to the billiard room and a patera inspired by a detail in the Villa Kérylos—a twentieth-century Greek-inspired residence on the French Riviera—found its way to the powder room. The varying backgrounds establish a unique experience in each space, yet one room isn't trying to outdo another by virtue of its virtuoso wall treatment. (Exception must be granted to the dining room, whose walls of hand-painted Gracie paper knock the others out of the park.)

Against these backdrops I hung window treatments that soften the spaces and provide an opportunity for color and visual interest. I commissioned master weavers in Laos to craft beautiful, subtle patterns into silk panels for the dining room. In the living room I installed ethereal curtains

OPPOSITE: The front door of the Mark Ferguson–designed house is reached through a colonnaded cloister. The design for the bronze lanterns is based on an antique fixture—sixteen were custom made for this space. FOLLOWING SPREAD: The entry foyer features an elaborately designed mosaic floor. The gilded mirrors and consoles are nineteenth-century Italian, and the vases are Murano glass and date to the 1930s. The gilt-bronze chandelier is by the noted American firm of Bradley and Hubbard Manufacturing Company and was made around 1920.

of unlined silk. The enormous arched doors don't require them for sun control, but the room would be far less elegant without the shimmering pale-blue draperies. A flat linen panel featuring an embroidered tree (another reference to the Villa Kérylos) hangs in the powder room. I incorporated simple trims, modest braids, and embroidered details along the drapery edges, and some windows feature sheer underlayments or shades of textured woven grass and matchsticks. None of the treatments are overly elaborate in their design, which keeps the rooms from becoming too fussy or formal.

My clients and I found much of the furniture while shopping together in San Francisco, New York, and Los Angeles. Every piece is exceptional in its own right, but we combined them in ways that allow all to relate. The eggshell-lacquer tray tables in the living room are from the 1930s but seem perfectly at ease juxtaposed against eighteenth-century Italian chairs. A contemporary bronze coffee table with gilt bronze bugs and birds by French artisan Paula Swinnen rests comfortably next to an early-nineteenth-century Italian secretary. The mix-and-match aesthetic—midcentury mated with eighteenth century—continues throughout the home in a manner that seems natural and not forced.

Given my predilection for antique and vintage lighting, it's no surprise that this house features a wide range of fixtures, and there are numerous examples of fabulous finds. The pair of eighteenth-century wood-and-iron lanterns that anchor the living room are truly spectacular, but no more so than the enormous Murano glass chandelier that hangs above the dining room table. I found a few antique pieces that I had reproduced, and some contemporary sconces are every bit as beautiful as their vintage counterparts. Each room displays what I consider to be an essential component—a decorative fixture—that serves to illuminate as well as accentuate the space's decor. Imagine how sad these rooms would appear if lit only by dreary recessed cans!

Ultimately this house—and the interiors—is the result of a truly collaborative effort. It's reflective of the clients' tastes, as well as their aesthetic inclinations and personal opinions. Their viewpoints and sentiments contributed as much as my own instincts and those of the architects. Throughout the process there was continuous communication among the design team, the parents, and their children, each participant striving to achieve the most beautiful outcome. Building the home was a family affair, and every point of view was considered and respected. (And only occasionally rejected!) It's quite a feat to have so many cooks in the kitchen and come out with such a delectable feast for the eyes.

OPPOSITE: A pair of eighteenth-century Tuscan lanterns hangs in the double-height living room. The furniture is a collection of antique and contemporary pieces, including custom-designed sofas, eighteenth-century Italian bergères, and a pair of brass tole lamps from the 1960s. The pair of white-bronze birds are 1930s Japanese. FOLLOWING SPREAD: The opposite end of the living room is anchored by a stunning pair of nineteenth-century Chinese screens depicting a mountain range. The carpet is an antique Oushak, and the tables in front of the sofa are made from 1930s eggshell-lacquer trays. The white vessel on the left table is Chinese, from the Southern Song dynasty (1127–1279).

ABOVE: A custom stencil pattern—hand-painted by Maria Trimbell and then heavily sanded away so it almost disappears—creates depth and warmth on the walls of the living room. OPPOSITE: The coffee table in the living room was made by French artisan Paula Swinnen and features birds, flowers, and an assortment of insects all rendered in gilt bronze. FOLLOWING SPREAD: The hand-painted Chinese wallpaper in the dining room provides a dramatic backdrop for a 1940s French console and a 1960s Murano chandelier. Two of the dining chairs are Danish and date to 1910—the rest are exact copies. PAGE 248: A detail of the dining room's hand-painted wallpaper with a 1960s Murano sconce. PAGE 249: The faience urn on the dining table is French circa 1900.

ABOVE AND OPPOSITE: The design for the powder room was inspired by the decorative motifs of the Villa Kérylos, the Greek Revival villa built in the South of France by Theodore Reinach circa 1908. The walls were hand-painted by Maria Trimbell, and the vintage solid-marble sink is from the 1930s. I designed the mosaic floor and had it made in Italy. FOLLOWING SPREAD: A capacious green linen-velvet L-shaped sofa is the centerpiece of the family room. The bronze-and-leather ottoman was custom made for the space, and the Italian chairs at right are from the 1950s. Two antique prayer shawls from Indonesia hang above a console table, at left. PAGES 254-55: The pergola seating area off the family room.

Classic faux-bamboo chairs surround a painted breakfast table modeled after a design by Jansen, the famed French decorating firm. The top of the table (above) is painted to look like marble.

OPPOSITE: The Japanese screen mounted on the library's walnut paneling appears contemporary but is actually from the Edo period (1603–1868). The glazed porcelain pail in the foreground is by noted Korean ceramicist Young Sook Park. FOLLOWING SPREAD: The library's massive alabaster table lamps were one of the first purchases for the house. They sit on purple parchment tables by Aldo Tura that date to the 1960s. The armchairs are French Art Deco, and the Creation of Man patinated-bronze coffee table is by Philip and Kelvin LaVerne.

RIGHT: The master bedroom is a soothing cocoon of silk textiles in various textures. Handwoven in Laos, a smooth patterned fabric is used on the custom gilded bed; the walls are covered in a silk strié; the window treatments are silk burlap panels with an embroidered border of our design; and the fabric for the chair and ottoman is a sumptuous cut-silk velvet. The painted and gilded sunburst above the bed is from a seventeenth-century Italian altarpiece. PAGE 264: The silk velvet on the armchair and ottoman was handwoven in Venice. PAGE 265: The Japanese-style console is covered in layers of linen, which was painted with gesso, allowed to dry, and then rolled, cracked, and ultimately lacquered to create texture and visual interest. The vintage Chinoiserie-style mirror is by Philip and Kelvin LaVerne. The vase is by Japanese ceramic artist Suzuki Souji.

ABOVE AND OPPOSITE: The two master bathrooms were designed as a study in contrasts. His bathroom features dark-stained walnut cabinetry and a boldly patterned marble floor. Her bathroom walls are covered in a hand-painted Chinese wallcovering that evokes a decidedly more feminine spirit. FOLLOWING SPREAD: In the seating area of the pool pergola, woven seagrass furniture surrounds a stone table. The vintage rope-covered chandelier served as inspiration for the custom-made sconces. The rear facade of the house is seen across the lawn.

ACKNOWLEDGMENTS

Without question my staunchest ally also happens to be the love of my life. My husband, Steve Oney, saw promise in me before I was able to see it in myself. He believed in me when I was floundering and recognized my talent and ability long before I did. He encouraged me to follow this path and has buoyed my confidence through difficult times (and difficult clients).

My mother, Harriet Stuart, is a force of nature and a constant source of inspiration. Her influence is unquestionable, and she continues to be the greatest champion of my work. I inherited my business instincts from my maternal grandmother, Rhea Dolin, but my eye for design and beauty was instilled by Harriet.

Nicole Yorkin, one of my dearest friends, receives full credit for launching my career. Her faith in me never wavered, even when I was struggling to find my way. She recommended me to Ed Solomon, my first client. And while I'm indebted to Ed for granting me the opportunity, Nicole is the one who never doubted my ability.

One of my earliest supporters was Margaret Russell. I walked into the offices of *Elle Decor* more than two decades ago, and she saw enough promise in the lousy scouting shots I'd brought along that she arranged to have my project photographed for the magazine. That story features a house I did for Lisa Henson—a client I still collaborate with some thirty years later. The images, photographed by the exceptionally talented Dominique Vorillon, look as fresh now as they did then. Margaret and Dominique became a part of my life on that shoot. I owe them a debt of gratitude for their efforts on my behalf all those years ago and for their friendship ever since.

Throughout my career I have learned from—and been inspired by—significant purveyors of beautiful objects. I have benefited immensely from their guidance, and although some of them have passed on, I continue to be grateful for the part they played in my life. Among the many I admire, there are a few to whom I'm most thankful for their friendship, support, and generosity. They include Joel Chen, Tommy Raynor, Adam Blackman, David Cruz, David Calligeros, Robert Willson, David Serrano, Christian Jaillite, Barbara Kirshbaum, Benjamin Izett, Amy Perlin, and the dealers Smith & Houchins and Evans & Gerst.

Without the talent, insight, and advice of the artisans and craftspeople who interpret my work, my accomplishments would be negligible. I am much obliged to those who have been at my side in the trenches, helping me execute and create what would otherwise be relegated to paper. I am beholden to Jean Horihata, Tom Roth, Wilfredo Flores, Ricardo Baca, Arturo Zelaya, Paul Martin, Tom Rogers, Victor Hernandez, Marc Dierickx, Alex Menegaz, Eddie and Romero Grana, Bryan Bobrosky, Duane Longworth, Gina and Natalie Berschneider, Donald Kaufman, and Taffy Dahl. Scores of others have helped me build, fabricate, and realize whatever I've imagined, and I thank them all.

I started out as a solo practitioner, and as my firm grew, so did my staff. This is a challenging business and it requires a devoted and dedicated team to ensure that ideas and designs are brought to life. Their efforts on my behalf—and that of our clients—are incalculable and greatly appreciated. There have been many who've aided and abetted me over the years, but there are a few who've actually changed my life. The list includes Alisa Milhollan, Tyler Colgan, Casey Goldstein, Janee Fraser, Amy Wolfe, Daniel Jones, and Valli Zale. Amy Flynn Socci deserves special mention for collaborating with me on some of our most beautiful work, and for her extraordinary assistance, fortitude, and support during the photo shoots for this book.

I've always loved designing furniture, and since 1995 I've produced my own line. It's an ambitious undertaking and requires the support of trade showrooms around the country. The Madeline Stuart Collection is represented by the best in the business: Dan Cahoon of Jerry Pair; Art Ellsworth and Marvin Wilkinson of John Brooks; the incomparable Thomas Lavin in Los Angeles and Laguna; and Hewn, where Peter West and Jeff Holt treat me like a rock star. I owe a special debt of gratitude to Geoff De Sousa and Eric Hughes, who were the first to believe in my endeavor.

Then there are my clients, without whom I wouldn't be able to practice what I preach and do what I love. You know who you are. Ed, Stacey, and Lisa started the ball rolling, and I tip my hat to them for taking a chance on a greenhorn decorator. Alex taught me to insist on slot-head screws. I discovered Lone Pine and Hawaii thanks to Sean and Ruthie, and fell in love with Wyoming and Montana because of Kelly and George. I've worked on some exceptional houses with marvelous clients and I am inordinately beholden to them all for their support and patronage. And to those who granted me permission to feature their houses in this book, I am forever grateful.

It was quite a few years ago that I told Jill Cohen I didn't think I was deserving of a book devoted to my work. Now I do. She has been an incredibly supportive part of this process, and I couldn't have done it without her help and insight. I am enormously indebted to Doug Turshen, David Huang, and Philip Reeser, who brought it all to life with their diligence, care, and respect for both my work and my words.

I've considered Mayer Rus a friend for more years than I care to admit. I admire him for his remarkable knowledge of design, art, and architecture and adore him for his wicked wit. I'm honored that he agreed to write the Foreword.

At every step of the way, this book has been a collaborative effort with the incomparably talented Trevor Tondro. Patience is one of his many virtues, and his eye for beauty and elegant simplicity is evident on every page. We started the conversation over boiled shrimp and white wine, and continued to eat and drink and laugh all the way through. His assistant extraordinaire, Kyle Petrozza, was there almost every step of the way, providing the soundtrack to our shoots and insisting the camera be in focus.

Lastly there are the artists who are part of my life, part of who I am. From David Bowie, I discovered the potential for reinvention; from Antonio Carlos Jobim, the power of *saudade*. I learned about color from Milton Avery and Edward Hopper and blackness from the canvases of John Singer Sargent and Diego Velázquez. I am affected every day by a piece of music or art and am blessed to have had parents who encouraged me to see and hear. I feel incredibly lucky that each venture affords me the opportunity to invent and explore a design vocabulary unique to that project and that every client pushes me to be a better designer than I was the day before. It has taken me many years to get to the point I'm at today—what compels me forward is to discover where I'll find myself tomorrow. As Shakespeare writes in *Hamlet*, "We know what we are but know not what we may be."

First published in the United States of America in 2019 by
Rizzoli International Publications, Inc.
300 Park Avenue South
New York, New York 10010
www.rizzoliusa.com

© 2019 by Madeline Stuart
Foreword: Mayer Rus
Text: Madeline Stuart
Photographs: Trevor Tondro

Publisher: Charles Miers
Editor: Philip Reeser
Design: Doug Turshen with David Huang
Production Manager: Barbara Sadick
Copy Editor: Elizabeth Smith
Managing Editor: Lynn Scrabis

Printed in China
2019 2020 2021 2022 / 10 9 8 7 6 5 4 3 2 1

ISBN: 978-0-8478-6357-0
Library of Congress Control Number: 2019932488

Visit us online:
Facebook.com/RizzoliNewYork
Twitter: @Rizzoli_Books
Instagram.com/RizzoliBooks
Pinterest.com/RizzoliBooks
Youtube.com/user/RizzoliNY
Issuu.com/Rizzoli